UPGRADE

10 Secrets to the Best Education for Your Child

Titles from Kevin Swanson

Family Bible Study Guides
Psalms I: A Family Bible Study Guide
Psalms II: A Family Bible Study Guide
Genesis: A Family Bible Study Guide
Proverbs: A Family Bible Study Guide

Christian Curriculum Project
Christian Classics Study Guide
Great Christian Classics: Five Great Narratives of the Faith
Christian Classics Study Guide – Junior Level

The Second Mayflower
Upgrade: 10 Secrets to the Best Education for Your Child

Vision for Generations (Mp3)
Vision for Generations (CD)
Reforming the Church in the 21st Century (CD)
*Family Economics Series—Building your Family Economy
(Mp3, CD, or DVD)*

UPGRADE

10 Secrets to the Best Education for Your Child

KEVIN SWANSON

GENERATIONS *WITH* VISION

ISBN: 978-0-9826298-4-0

Published by
Generations with Vision
10431 South Parker Road
Parker, Colorado, 80134
www.generationswithvision.com

For more information on this and
other titles from Generations with Vision,
visit www.generationswithvision.com or call 1-888-839-6132.

CONTENTS

Introduction

If you are a parent and you have purchased this book with an interest in providing the best education possible for your child, then we are already in agreement on the central thesis of the book. The thesis is that parents have a committed interest in their children's education; and they must, therefore, be equipped to make intelligent, well-informed choices concerning that education.

There are not many topics more important than education in our world today. It is the issue that you will always find near the top of the brochures pitching political candidates. When every other tax initiative fails to gain popular support, the voting public enthusiastically endorses increased taxes to fund some new educational institution or program. The incorrigible assumption clinging to the minds of the voters is that more tax money will solve all of our education problems.

There is a growing dissatisfaction with the condition of education in many industrialized countries today. The concern has some scientific merit. Recent studies comparing the academic performance of school children from various nationalities in the areas of math and science put America into the ranks of third-world nations (still beating out nations like Mozambique and Jordan, but well below Spain, Hungary, and China).[1] Of eighteen industrialized nations, the Organization for Economic Cooperation and Development recently found the United States ranked dead last in the literacy of sixteen- to twenty-five-year-old high school graduates.[2] For the last six years, I have worked at an office that receives thousands of phone calls each year from parents who are greatly dissatisfied with the education their children receive from their local publicly funded school district. Parents are rightfully concerned. The statistics illustrate one thing, but there are deeper problems. School violence is on the rise. Negative social influences abound in many schools, causing parents even more distress. Businesses are concerned about the less-than-competent workforce emerging from the high schools and colleges in our country. A decline in academic achievement will inevitably affect our economy, our national defense, and the American way of life.

The most frightening truth that a parent might occasionally assume courage to face is this: Our children *could really suffer* from a low-quality educational experience. It is even possible *to fail* in the raising of children. While every child is responsible for his own actions, it is true that some approaches have been much more effective than others in the training and education of a child. There are children in this world who, for one reason or another, do not receive a good upbringing or a good education. Nevertheless, this is not always the end of the story. Some of these children are able, by God's grace, to transcend dysfunctional early years and excel in life. However, this is much more the exception than the rule.

The chief purpose of this book is not to critique the present system, but rather to present the positive factors that really do work to produce a quality education. There has been much written on the problems with our modern public school system. Reforms are constantly recommended. Hardly a year goes by without the implementation of new reforms and remedies in this nation's schools. My purpose here is not to recommend a reform program for the nation. My purpose is simply to inform, involve, and equip parents with a basic knowledge of the principles upon which a quality education must be built.

INTRODUCTION

There are *hundreds* of different approaches to education. For parents and teachers alike, experts are plentiful across the academic landscape. Contradicting theories abound. The cacophony of competing messages confuse and frustrate us. We throw our hands up and assign the whole thing to professionals, who appear to know what they are doing. But they are just as confused as the rest of us.

There are two explanations for the proliferation of perspectives on education. The first is that some approaches taken are just *plain wrong* and will not work. Somehow we have been trained in this modern age to believe that all new ideas are inherently good. This line of thinking has corrupted education more than anything else; and many of us are growing tired of the new theories, new math, new philosophies, and new reforms. When it comes to the basic issues of life, when it comes to something as important as educating our children, new is risky. New is *not* tried and true. It is essential to build on the principles that are time-tested, tried-and-true.

Some educational theories are wrongheaded because they are mistaken at the root. For example, one person might say there is no God, while another claims there is a God. They cannot both be right. One of them is terribly mistaken. One person might claim that children are basically good, while another claims that children have a sinful nature. Again, they cannot both be right. The method of education for children usually rests on certain basic philosophical perspectives. A method will be developed according to the foundational worldview perspective held by those who administer, teach, or write textbooks. Not every worldview is of equal merit. Some worldview perspectives hold a wrong position on such important questions as the existence of God, the nature of man, the essential value of man, his purpose in life, and so on. Since there are conflicting worldviews, there will be radically differing ideas concerning the education of children. Those who build an educational approach on the wrong worldview will produce a bad education.

The second explanation for the proliferation of approaches in education is found in the principle of individuality (a principle considered in chapter 6). Since every child is an individual, there are some methods that *will* work with some children, while they simply *will not* work with others. This means that the method of education may vary depending on the culture, the school, the families, or the children. We are not arguing for uniformity here. On the contrary, we want to protect and nurture diversity in educational methods while, at the same time, maintaining the universal, basic principles of education.

The fundamental assumption I have taken in this presentation is that there is a God who created the world. Thankfully, he provided a basic operating manual for life — the Bible. It establishes for us an absolute point of reference. Without it, we would be wandering in a blinding snowstorm of relativism without any hope of distinguishing between a good education and a bad education. The principles we will consider in this book are rooted in the revelation provided in the Bible. I would argue that one must take into full consideration the truth about reality revealed by the God who made reality before applying the principles to any specific school or to the education of any child. Moreover, this revelation from the Old and New Testaments bears the time-tested quality that is so needed today. *Why would anyone embark on a study of something as important as education without taking into consideration the rich historical writings of the ancient Jews and Christians?*

There is a great deal more to say about education than what is contained in these pages. The reason for leaving this material out is twofold. First, I wanted to write a short book. Secondly, the other concepts are not *basic principles*. They do not hold the indispensable quality that the ten principles hold. They do not have the time-tested quality that is provided in the book of wisdom thousands of years old, given by revelation from God. What we cover here are the principles that must be taken into account by any parent who is choosing an educational program for his or her child. Individuality forces the door open for a great number of approaches. The methodology used for one student might differ quite radically from another, but each of the principles contained in this book ought to be conscientiously integrated into the education of every single child. While some ideas may have more or less validity in any particular case, there are certain universal principles that are unchanging across time and space. They have been given by God himself. This book provides the basics of education that are just as relevant and applicable to a first-century Hebrew child as they are to a twenty-first-century Japanese girl or for a twenty-eighth-century boy from the southern state of Mississippi.

This book will address the highest-order principles for education. For example, chapter 10 explains the principle of the honor and mystique of learning. While there are others that might develop *how* the honor and mystique is established in the classroom or the homeschool, the *how* will often be different depending on the cultures and settings in which education occurs. The principles in this book are indispensable yet broad principles. If one cannot see these ten large girders in the building of education, he will not be able to master the building of an education.

There are some who study the principles of teaching for six to ten years in under-graduate, graduate, and post-graduate university programs. Although I cannot give my reader a doctorate in education in this very short presentation, I submit that one does not have to have a doctorate in education to be an excellent teacher. Anyone who has the ability to communicate can be a mentor, a discipler, a master, or a teacher. Anyone who maximizes on the principles contained in this book in the education or discipleship of a child will maximize the development of that child's potential.

This book is written *by* a parent primarily *for* parents. While the material contained here is basic for all educators, it is parents who have the deepest interest in their children's intellectual, emotional, and spiritual development. Parents are, beyond all other interests, responsible for their children's training and development. If parents are intimately familiar with the eternal, universal principles of a good education, then they will be able to apply these principles in their selection of an effective educational program for their children. It is not the purpose of this book to define the exact dimensions, shape, and color of that program. The program will take on a different shape for different cultures, different families, and different children within those families. But parents are encouraged to take the ten universal, unchanging principles of education and apply them to their unique culture, family, and children.

This author has been part of the modern home education movement for thirty-five years—as a student, parent/teacher, and leader in the movement. Having taught in various state schools and private schools, junior high through college, I have seen every one of the ten principles used successfully by various teachers in various situations. Many good educators, including many home educators, will center in on one or two of the principles and base an entire philosophy of education or curriculum on those factors. Although they are not always aware of what they are doing, every good educator usually employs these factors in their teaching to some degree or another. It is rare, however, to find any school, teacher, or parent in the present day who self-consciously employs all ten factors.

This book is *not* meant to recommend for every child any particular institution of education, whether it be public school, private school, or homeschool. Parents must make their own informed choices. Nevertheless, their choices should incorporate *all ten* of these indispensable elements of a quality education. Every parent and teacher who happens to be holding this book is challenged to take, apply, and maximize these ten critical factors in the educational program put together for each of the children in their charge.

A Successful Education 1

I was an expert in child training and education—that is, until the day our first child arrived. In God's infinite wisdom, he sent us a little boy who, upon emerging from the womb, was screaming. He screamed for the next two years, only taking occasional breaks to eat and sleep. The experience was instantly humbling for this particular "expert." Since then, my wife and I have found there are no child-raising experts—except One. There is no silver bullet that solves all problems for all children. Looking back over the last thirteen years, perhaps the most valuable lesson learned was that child raising is a process—one that demands great love, patience, wisdom, and humility from parents. I learned right away that some children are not a mere 30 percent more difficult than others at certain times in their lives. Some children are *one hundred times* more difficult than other children. Occasionally I have seen a parent of a smart, easy-going, motivated child approach a family who is struggling every day with an energetic, slow-learning, intensely emotional, and willful child to offer some little piece of sage advice. The incongruity is almost humorous. These well-meaning counselors soon discover that the parents of the little wildcat are doing the right things. They may be a little frazzled around the edges, but they are doing the right things. Any expert who promises instant success if you use some neat little recipe in the training or educating of a child either has never had the blessing of raising a tornado

7

or has never had children at all. The timeless principles of child raising and education will only work over the long haul, and the true success of that education can only be measured by the results in the long run.

When those little ones show up in our lives, they come with "some assembly required." Every parent quickly discovers that these little ones start out in life with a propensity for sticking pudgy little fingers into electrical sockets, for uncontrolled screaming, and for copious leaking. For some reason God designed children such that they require an investment of certain things into their lives. It was his intent that we develop these beautiful creatures, created in his image, that they might further reflect his glory in life and eternity. That is the role of education.

So, education is vitally important to the life of every single child. There is hardly a politician, teacher, or parent alive who would not agree. But if everyone considers education to be all that important, what is education? If you are after a successful education for your child, it would make sense to first define what it is that makes an education.

I define education this way:

> *Education is the preparation of a child intellectually, emotionally,*
> *spiritually, and physically for life and for eternity.*

A Broad Definition

A striking element of a definition like this is that it is very broad. It might include child training, discipline, academics, socialization, and every possible experience a child will meet with in his developing years.

A common misconception of education comes when the definition of education narrows to the intellectual. The child is compartmentalized. He is not seen as a whole person, fully integrated with physical, emotional, spiritual, and intellectual capacities. Thus, if an educational program attempts to address the child's intellect while ignoring his spiritual and emotional development, the approach is sadly ignoring the true reality of the child. Likewise, those who separate the spiritual and emotional part of the child from the intellectual make a big mistake. You cannot delegate only the intellectual training of your child to professionals and retain just the spiritual and emotional development for yourself. Whatever class is taught, the whole child is affected. Physical education (P.E.), for example, does focus on the physical part of the child, but the emotional and intellectual sides are also affected (in the locker room or out on the field). And anyone who thinks that a student develops only intellectual maturity in an algebra class has never taught algebra!

Education Is *Paideia*

"And fathers . . . bring [your children] up in the training (paideia) *and instruction* (nouthesia) *of the Lord." Ephesians 6:4*

This is the key New Testament passage relating to the raising of children. The key word in this key passage is *paideia*. This Greek word used by Paul in his first-century epistle was as common then as our word *democracy* is today. It was a word that carried extensive connotation. *Paideia* was the entire process whereby the ideal citizen was raised for the ideal state. It involved far more than the stack of books assigned to a child at the beginning of the school year. It included every input and influence that came into the child's life (such as peers, games, a geography textbook, novels, and chores). Paideia is the development of a child from a baby to a man or a woman. Of course, Paul used the word in a different sense than the pagan Greeks of his time. He spoke of raising the child in the *paideia* "of the Lord." Christians raise their children in the *paideia* of Christ.

Worldview Considerations

Another observation warranted by the above definition of education is that our worldview, our fundamental view of reality, is going to affect our understanding of education. Education differs according to one's view of such things as God and eternity. Education will be very different if a child is *not* being prepared for eternity. If, however, the human soul survives physical death, then the preparation a child receives here on Earth will impact his eternal state. One who has been prepared with a view to eternity will learn to make decisions in life in light of eternity. For example, he will learn to tell the truth, even though it may be disadvantageous in the short term.

Preparation

Education is defined as *preparation,* but preparation for what? There must be some purpose toward which that preparation is directed. The classic Old Testament text encouraging parents to provide an education for their children is Deuteronomy 6:6–9. Thankfully, this passage is prefaced with the main content of that education, the purpose for which that child will live his life: "Love the LORD your God with all your heart, with all your soul, and with all your strength" (v. 5). Every child will also have a unique calling for which he must be prepared. This usually involves work, a future marriage, and a future home. Sometimes it includes positions of high responsibility and leadership. In the case of children with special needs, this preparation may call for a great amount of faith and wisdom. Parents must recognize the inherent value of the child in this life, especially in terms of the relationships he will cultivate. But even more important is the fact that our children are being prepared for a calling in eternity.

Each child has a specific calling, framed by his unique talents and abilities. This we would draw from the principle of individuality (1 Thess. 4:11 and 1 Cor. 12:17–31, presented in more detail in chapter 6). Every child is created with unique gifts for a unique calling. It is a common mistake to reduce these callings to intellectual gifts, which happens when you conclude that some children are gifted in math, others are gifted in writing, and others are not gifted in any intellectual pursuit. Everybody is gifted and has a purpose in God's world. Some gifts may lie in the arena of the spiritual, emotional, or physical more than the intellectual.

The challenge of the first eighteen years of a child's education is to find that calling. One thing we can safely say is that every child is called to a life of glorifying God and enjoying him (1 Cor. 10:31). That is the first level of purpose. After that we begin to note distinctive callings. The first difference you will note between children in the determination of calling is *gender*. This should be an obvious difference, though it is sadly ignored in many cases today. After taking account of gender differences, each child's calling will then depend on the gifts and abilities that God has given him.

When a child is young, his calling may be defined in broad terms. For example, one might determine that the child needs to know how to use the restroom, purchase groceries, and read the Bible. As he grows older, it is crucial that more specificity be added to that calling. Efforts must be taken in the high-school years to flesh out the calling for each individual child. What a tragedy to find twenty-eight-year-old men wandering about from college program to college program, from career track to career track, searching for a calling. From the time a child is twelve years old, serious efforts must be taken by parents and child alike to narrow in on that calling. Part-time jobs, apprenticeships, tours of work sites, counseling, and testing[1] should be incorporated into those key developmental years. A much wider selection of special elective courses should be made available to the teenage high-school student. Parents should be intimately involved as counselors in this focusing process. Who knows the student better than his parents? A fulfilled life will be determined to a great extent by whether or not a man or woman has centered in upon his or her life calling. How many midlife crises could be avoided if this were taken seriously in the teenage years!

Preparation of What?

The *whole* child must be prepared for his calling. The child is more than a brain. Certainly at two years of age a child is not ready to go to work and establish a household. There is much development that must occur. His intellect, body, emotions, and soul must be prepared for the challenges that will make up that calling God has placed on his life. The emotions are prepared for the complex emotional challenges he will face in his calling. Those callings that involve more emotional strength will require stronger emotional preparation. Those callings that involve more intellectual development in some area (such as law, medicine, or engineering) will require a higher level of preparation in that particular area.

A Successful Education

As we grapple with the definition of education, we must also consider the matter of a successful education. If education involves preparation for future life, it stands to reason that we would want a successful life; and a successful education would seek that end.

Interestingly, there is a disconnection today between modern college education and the business world. Many corporations are forced to provide extensive in-house training programs to produce effective employees, for both blue-collar and white-collar jobs. This disconnection is even more pronounced in the K-12 academic world. It is conspicuous in a humorous quip commonly used in the entrepreneurial world of millionaires: "A-students end up teaching, and B-students end up working for C-students."

While there is no way this quip could be supported by empirical studies as a universal rule, there is evidence indicating that grades have little to do with success in the business world. The research conducted by Dr. Tom Stanley on 733 millionaires proves just this point. The factors of high intelligence quotients and high academic grades showed up near the bottom of the list of those factors contributing to business success; while honesty, self-discipline, hard work, socialization skills, and career fit (or calling) scored at the top of the list.[2]

Robert Kiyosaki, author of *Rich Dad's Cashflow Quadrant*, insists that it "does not take a good formal education [to make money]. I have a college degree and I can honestly say that achieving financial freedom had nothing to do with what I learned in college."[3] Among those who did not acquire a college degree before achieving outstanding success are Thomas Edison, Henry Ford, Bill Gates, Ted Turner, Michael Dell, Steve Jobs, and Ralph Lauren. The reasons behind the disconnection between the business world and the academic world will be thoroughly explored in the remainder of this book as we review the factors that contribute to a successful education.

But what about a successful education? Is success strictly measured by monetary gain, a notion that seems to be pressed upon us by a materialist age? Does success for a child who achieves a perfect score on the Scholastic Aptitude Test mean the same thing as success for a child with Down's Syndrome who may never leave his parents' home? What is success in the education of a child?

Success in education cannot be confined to academics. Indeed, a child might be very smart yet never learn to stay focused and motivated on a life's calling. A child might have an outstanding technical ability but use it to crack safes and rob banks. Success must include spiritual and emotional maturity. For parents of faith, the passing along of that faith to the next generation is of great value. In most cases, a successful raising will produce a young man or woman able to lead a family. Successive generations will then be better prepared for life than the previous ones.

In the ultimate sense, only God can define success for us because only God can identify the ultimate purpose for man. Therefore, success must have something to do with a child raised in the "*paideia* of God," whether or not that child becomes a millionaire or a great leader. God's method means success only because God's method is designed to deliver God's purposes. I define a successful education as follows:

A successful education is achieved when a child is prepared to make maximal use of his God-given talents and abilities in the accomplishment of the child's calling.

Generally speaking, the success of a family (a husband and a wife) that is effective in the calling to which God has brought them is manifest in some material blessing. This material success is usually seen in terms of growth in net worth or an expansion of the initial capital investments of inheritance or educational training. But this is not true in every case. Some who have achieved material success have done so without exercising their respective callings. Conversely, others have exercised their respective callings with great care and diligence without any tangible material success.

What is assumed in a definition of success is that which is proposed here—the recognition and maximum use of a person's gifts and abilities. It is vital to have a vision for the *paideia* of a child if you want to achieve anything approaching success. If you have no objective for which you are preparing your child, you will never achieve any appreciable success. Therefore, the first measure of success would have to be found in the identification of the calling and the first implementation of it in something like a first business venture or apprenticeship.

Successful preparation for a calling must also involve a full-orbed scope, including an emotional confidence, a spiritual faith and character, and an intellectual and physical equipping targeted for the particular calling that has been chosen.

This preparation must include an element of motivation and focus. If the specific vision conveyed to a young person does not produce some degree of focus and motivation towards that calling, one must conclude that either the calling was not chosen correctly or the preparation was inadequate. If the calling is properly selected, the young person should come to realize, "This is where I fit." He or she will retain a measure of confidence and motivation to keep moving in the general direction of the calling.

Conclusion

As we will discover later in this book, the success of education cannot be limited to a quarterly report card. The success of education cannot be measured by education itself. The capstone of education is found in the implementation of a calling. Education is preparation for life, so life is the only real measure of the success of education. That is why success has a great deal to do with the *successful exercise of one's gifts and abilities in life itself.* Without this objective measure, the progress of education will be measured the same way the emperor monitored the progress of his new clothes makers! Therefore, success in education must be seen in broad terms, which does not eliminate the precious child with special needs who never exceeds a "third-grade" level of learning. Success in education will be seen in the success of relationships, the success of a spiritual journey, the success of a marriage, the success of a family, the success of a business, and the success of career and investments over an entire lifetime. It will be seen in young men and young women who find where they fit in life. It will be seen in those who learn to love the Lord their God with all their heart, soul, mind, and strength. It will be seen in those who have learned to glorify God, enjoy him, obey him, and worship him. Ultimately, that success will be seen in eternity.

2 The Data on Education:
What Every Parent Needs to Know

According to the results from nationally standardized tests taken by American school children, some forms of education work better than others. The studies alone cannot recommend one educational approach for every single child on the face of the earth. This is because of the principle of individuality. Also, one must remember that no scientific study is definitive. There is always a margin of error. Moreover, these studies typically compare the averages in the study group and do not consider the whole distribution of the range. When you look at the academic performance of a group of students on a standardized test, the data make up a bell curve. Many of the students will be grouped around an average, while a few students fall at the high and low ends of the spectrum. Each child is an individual, and some children may perform well in one environment and not in another. There are other factors that contribute to the success or failure of a student (besides the factors looked at in one particular study). These factors might include the quality of parenting, economic conditions, intellectual ability of the student, and so forth. Scientific studies can identify areas in which there are problems and areas in which we might look for solutions, but the studies hold no ultimate answers. This is why most of this book will be concerned with the principles of good education established by historical example and biblical revelation.

A Major Study

Twenty years ago, only 16 percent of Americans considered homeschooling a good idea. A radical shift has occurred in the American view of homeschooling since then. According to a recent poll, the percentage has risen to 42 percent.[1] Undoubtedly, the media has made a strong contribution to this change. Over the last several years, the majority of media coverage of homeschooling has been positive. Recently, homeschooled youngsters dominated the national spelling bee, taking home all three of the top prizes. In the national geography bee last year, three of the top six winners were homeschoolers. Homeschoolers are capturing 10 percent of the top full-ride college scholarships, yet they make up only 1 to 2 percent of the high-school graduates.[2] Homeschoolers are scoring well over the national average in nationally standardized tests, including the S.A.T. and A.C.T. college entrance exams.

Perhaps the most interesting educational study conducted in the last decade was performed by Dr. Lawrence Rudner and the E.R.I.C. Clearinghouse, involving more than twenty-one thousand homeschooled students. The study, analyzing student performance on standardized tests, found that the average homeschooled eighth-grade student tested four grade levels above the national average.[3] On average, homeschoolers tested above their public and private school counterparts in every grade and in every subject. The average scores of home-educated students in various subjects and grades ranked between the 75th and 85th percentiles.

The strongest piece of analysis coming from the Rudner study considered the performance of homeschooled children according to the number of years they had been homeschooled. The data showed that students who had been homeschooled *four years or longer* exhibited the greatest difference (in higher scores) over national average scores. Evidently, *sustained improvement* relies on a commitment to the process.

This does not mean that homeschooling is for everyone. Neither does it mean that everyone who homeschools does a good job. Every distribution has what statisticians call "the lower tail," and that would include the academic performance of homeschoolers. While some score in the 80th percentile, there are also those who score in the 10th to 20th percentile.

In 2009, Dr. Brian Ray from NHERI (the National Home Education Research Institute), conducted another significant study on the academic performance of home educated students in this country. Over the previous decade, the homeschool population had doubled, producing a wider distribution of participants in the movement, so of course academic leaders were interested in the results of this study, which included in excess of 12,000 students over a wider variety of testing services. The results are contained in the chart below.

Average Percentile (National Average—50 percentile)[4]

	2009 Ray Study	1999 Rudner Study
Reading	89	85
Language	84	73
Math	84	77

This data indicates a substantial improvement over the previous study conducted ten years earlier, with the most significant improvement seen in the areas of language and mathematics.

Compare this study also to a significant study just issued by Stanford's Center for Research on Education Outcomes on Charter School performance. The study of collective reading and math progress in 2,403 charter schools in 15 states and cities, including the District of Columbia, that was released in June, 2009, showed that almost half of the charter schools produced results similar to those from comparable public schools. Charter schools producing worse results than the traditional schools outnumbered those with better numbers by more than 2 to 1.

Factors That Do Not Contribute to Success or Failure

Nevertheless, a study of this magnitude demonstrating such outstanding results cannot be ignored. This should direct the attention of every school administrator, teacher, and parent in America toward the homeschooling option. What is it that homeschooling parents are doing *right*? Is it simply sitting at home and being taught by parents that brings out in children the kind of success seen in the Rudner study and substantiated by dozens of other studies?[5] Or is it something else?

These studies have found that there are a number of things that *do not contribute* to the success of the homeschool. For example, there is no statistically significant difference between the performance of homeschooled children with teacher-certified parents and those whose parents do not have teacher certification. Moreover, there was little significant difference between the performance of homeschooled children whose parents had doctoral and master's degrees versus those parents with only a high-school diploma. The data also seem to indicate that the economic status and race of the parents has little to do with the academic performance of a child. Interestingly, the same cannot be said for children enrolled in public schools. Students who attend conventional state schools and whose parents have master's and doctoral degrees perform at a significantly higher level than children whose parents do not have high-school diplomas.[6] In addition, parental economic status, race, and teacher certification remain more significant factors for those children attending the conventional state schools.

More Interesting Data

According to data recently obtained from the U.S. Department of Education, students enrolled in private schools perform higher on National Assessment of Educational Progress (NAEP) tests than do those from public schools.[7]

National Assessment and Evaluation Program Results Public vs. Private Schools

		Grade 4	Grade 8	Grade 12
Science				
	Public School	148	149	145
	Private School	163	166	161
Math				
	Public School	226	274	300
	Private School	238	287	315

Another recent study indicates that children tend to perform better in smaller schools than in larger schools.[8] While a number of studies have not indicated that a reduction of class size contributes to higher test scores, at least one study showed modest gains in performance for the early grades.[9] Most recent studies indicate that the quality of student performance in state schools has much to do with the quality of the teachers in those schools; however, what makes for quality teachers is a matter of debate and is difficult to analyze.[10]

The problem with these studies is that they do not flesh out the *reasons* why smaller schools are better than larger schools, or why homeschoolers tend to out-perform children enrolled in private or public schools. Therefore, pulling your children out of larger schools and placing them in smaller schools, private schools, or homeschools may not improve the situation for your particular children.

We live in the data age, the scientific age. We trust data, but we do not always interpret the data well. That is because everybody interprets data in light of their worldview framework. Besides this, every researcher has his or her biases that eventually determine how the study will be conducted, which factors will be analyzed, which will be blocked, and which will be ignored.

Even if we accept the results at face value, the studies are still based on "nationally standardized tests." These tests are incapable of determining the overall success of the education program over the life of one particular student. *Success* is a slippery term that is defined on the basis of one's worldview assumptions. The definition of success given in the first chapter simply cannot be tested by any of the nationally standardized exams presently used.

Conclusion

So why look at the data at all? The data can redirect our attention back into a general area that we have failed to consider. Scientific studies can force us to reevaluate our precommitments. They can force us to reevaluate the ancient method of home education and the principles behind it that make it work. After all, something must have worked with George Washington, Thomas Jefferson, James Madison, Theodore Roosevelt, Abraham Lincoln, Patrick Henry, Robert E. Lee, C. S. Lewis, Thomas Edison, Benjamin Franklin, Douglas MacArthur, Wolfgang Amadeus Mozart, and Charles Dickens. Each was homeschooled in his early years by father, mother, or both. What is it that these fathers and mothers did in their homes that proved to be effective? Did they capture the time-tested secrets of a successful education for their children?

This book is not meant to sell homeschooling as the only approach to education. Yet, there must be something operating in a homeschool far more effective than a five-year teaching degree, that produces such outstanding results. What is happening in the homeschool that takes the national average

21

for test scores sitting at the 50th percentile and ratchets it up 20 to 30 percentile points?

At a time when American education has seen a sharp decline in academic performance, home education is doing something right. There is something about homeschooling that *works*. What are those factors that produce such incredible success? Many of the factors for success in education discussed in this book are predominant in most homeschooling environments. At the same time, these factors appear to a far lesser extent in the conventional school environments. If we refuse to learn from others who are doing something with relative success, we are doomed to fail.

The First Time-Tested Secret for a Successful Education:

The Preeminence of Character

It was the dead of winter in the year 2000. My wife, Brenda, was three months pregnant with our fifth child. We had been changing diapers for close to eight years without a break, and we thought it would be nice to have a break. But there was one thing that stood in the way—potty training our fourth child, Bethany. We woke up one Saturday morning and determined that this was the day.

Every parent who trains a child to "go on the potty" learns something about education. Potty training is close to the first academic lesson a child must learn. She must make the connection between the urge "to go" and the potty chair. We set the arrangement up in the kitchen. For a good part of the day we explained this connection, spraying water into the chair, singing the little songs, explaining, coaxing, and pleading, but to no avail. She would sit pompously on her little throne for thirty minutes without any perceptible activity, then get up and go in her pants within two minutes. This was pretty much the routine for the day. As I was changing her clothes for the umpteenth time, I happened to notice that she was resisting my attempts to dress her. Then it hit me: maybe this child's problem was not physical or intellectual at all. Maybe the problem we were dealing with was a character problem.

Difficult though it may be to admit, my wife and I are not perfect parents; we go through periods where we are less than consistent at training. Knowing this, I suggested to my wife that we drop the potty-training bit and just focus on training our little one in that most basic character trait of all—respect and obedience to parents. We agreed that for one week we would focus not on potty training but on the all-important lesson of obedience.

What happened next forever changed our perspective of parenting. What we thought was shaping up to be the most difficult potty-training challenge we'd ever faced turned out to be the easiest. And it wasn't until we addressed the character issue that she was ready for the academic lesson of potty training. The child was potty-trained the very next day. She had trained herself.

The First Time-Tested Secret for a Successful Education: Preeminence of Character

Not everyone is equally enthusiastic about the character factor in education. Some of today's politicians do not agree that character is of basic and instrumental importance to career success or to the *paideia* of a child. They may conclude that character is of some importance—just as brushing your teeth for five minutes a day is important for healthy living—so they tack a perfunctory fifteen-minute class addressing the issue of character onto the end of Friday afternoon classes at the local state school. While it is hard for them to deny the importance of character, it is far easier to ignore it or minimize it, especially in the education of a child. The more practical area of character training tends to get lost while schools work hard to transfer long strings of facts into the child's mind.

Several years ago I began to seriously consider the question of whether the Bible had anything to say about education. If God designed the world and humankind and revealed something about the way the world functions, then most certainly he included something in this ancient Book as important as the preparation of little men and women for life and eternity. If the Bible included some content on the education of a child, what would it be? One way I found to identify biblical material on children was to perform a simple concordance search on the words *son* and *child*. Immediately, I discovered that an entire book of the Bible—the book of Proverbs—is dedicated to the subject of education. This entire book chronicles a father's training of his son—with the exception of the last chapter: mom's instructions to her son.

After making this discovery, I immediately recognized a problem. If Proverbs is the textbook for the education of a child, then isn't it strange that there is little about geography, geology, and geometry in this book? Why would God permit such a gross oversight in such an important book? Nevertheless, if we are to assume that God knew what he was doing when he inspired the book of Proverbs, then there must be a reason why he chose not to emphasize certain material. That reason is: the facts of geography, geology, and geometry *must not be all that important* in the education of a child. In fact, character is the foundation and structure of education. If education were a house, character would be the concrete foundation, the structure, the studs, and the drywall. Geography, geometry, and geology would be nothing but wallpaper. Of course it is the wallpaper that makes the house beautiful, attractive, and livable; but if it were not for the structure, there would be nothing on which the wallpaper could hang! Geography, geometry, and geology cannot be the substance of education. If character—the substance of education—is missing, then there is nothing upon which the rest of it can hang.

The content of Proverbs deals with the issues of character and faith. Character traits are seen in the various experiences and relationships in life—whether it be work, family, eating and drinking, marriage, or conflict. A careful study of the book of Proverbs identifies nine major themes of the book:

1. The Principle of the Tongue and the Truth

2. The Principle of Hard Work

3. The Principle of Self-Control and Avoiding Temptation

4. The Principle of Conflict Resolution and Getting Along with Others

5. The Principle of Fearing God

6. The Principle of Receiving Reproof and Respecting Authority

7. The Principle of Trusting God

8. The Principle of Humility

9. The Principle of the Virtuous Spouse

Successful Businessmen Agree

Dr. Thomas Stanley, a man who has dedicated his life to researching successful businessmen in America, has written a series of books on these millionaires. Although he does not refer to the Bible or the book of Proverbs in his discussion of success factors, his research correlates with the wisdom contained in that ancient book. In a survey of 733 millionaires,[1] Dr. Stanley found five factors to be most important to success in life:

1. Telling the Truth

2. Self-discipline

3. Getting Along with People

4. Having a Supportive Spouse

5. Hard Work

The number one factor claimed by millionaires to have contributed to success is "telling the truth." It is interesting to note that when I did a statistical survey on the lessons most frequently taught in the book of Proverbs, the most repeated character theme—mentioned more than 140 times—is honesty and the use of the tongue. An incredible coincidence? The next four factors on the millionaires' list are also prominent lessons in the book of Proverbs.

What about a supportive spouse? Of course that is the topic of the last chapter of the book:

> *Who can find a capable wife? She is far more precious than jewels. The heart of her husband trusts in her, and he will not lack anything good. She rewards him with good, not evil, all the days of her life.*
>
> *Proverbs 31:10–12*

I must point out, of course, that economic success is only one blessing among many potential blessings that attend a nation that upholds the character traits and lessons taught in the Proverbs. Moreover, not everyone who cultivates strength of character in his life is fabulously wealthy. Also, there are some very rich people who refuse to incorporate these characteristics into their lives; however, this kind of wealth is inevitably short-lived and usually disappears within a generation.

So Why Is Character So Important?

Why make such a big deal out of character? What is it about character that is so important to the process of educating a child? First, it should be obvious that intelligence alone will not produce a good person. You may have the smartest child in the world and put a lot of facts about chemistry and geography in his head, but he could grow up to be a smart terrorist who builds high-tech bombs that destroy innocent people.

Second, there are many smart children who grow up and simply cannot function. When I worked as a manager in the corporate world, I found that employees would seldom be fired for lack of brains. It was those who never learned the character traits of self-discipline, proper submission to authority, conflict resolution skills, or hard work who would receive their walking papers. The applicants who never learned how to "get along in the sandbox" would be the ones passed over time and again for a position or promotion.

Third, the process of education itself requires character. If a child has never learned to be self-disciplined, conscientious, patient, honest, and respectful of authority, it is doubtful he will ever be able to advance well in his academic studies. He cannot sit down and do the work. An extraordinarily sharp child may succeed in one particular course of study; but if he has a problem with slothfulness, he will fail to succeed when he runs into an obstacle. The best characterization of the sluggard is that which Proverbs provides. It describes the man who refuses to go out into the street for fear of the remote possibility of a lion attack. The sluggard is the man who refuses to act in the face of perceived or real obstacles (Prov. 22:13; 26:13).

The Uniqueness of Proverbs

It is true that many religions do recommend some form of character, including Confucianism, Buddhism, and Mohammedanian. More than a few schools include character development or some aspect of character in their mission statements and monikers. But underlying the entire book of Proverbs is a basic conception of God and a relationship with him. The Jehovah of Proverbs is sovereign; he is love, a Judge of hearts, and a Savior (Prov. 21:1; 15:9; 16:4–5; 18:10; 21:2). All the way through the book, the wise man assumes a relationship with God and recommends a disposition of reverent fear of God (1:9; 9:10; 15:33), rooted in a trust of him (3:5–6). True character and wise living will rise out of this disposition.

The First Character Lesson

The first character lesson for every child from the first day of his life is the lesson of honor, or reverent fear, of parents. Honor and reverent fear? Imagine watching a documentary on a national television network on the reverent fear and honor of parents! They are strange words indeed to the ears of a culture that has wandered far from the trait. Nevertheless, this is the ancient commandment given directly to *children*. Success in life, including success in academics, is hinged on this character trait. "Honor your father and mother . . . that it may go well with you." It is the first commandment with promise (Eph. 6:1–2; Exod. 20:12; Lev. 19:3).

Actually, the most commonly used characterization of a wise person in Proverbs is one who has learned to receive reproof and instruction from a superior (Prov. 1:5; 9:8–9; 10:8; 12:1; 15:5; 15:31; 17:10). The student must learn to walk in the path of obedience and submission, outlined in Proverbs 4:1–10. First he listens to his father (v. 1). Then he learns to aggressively *pursue* his father's wisdom (vv. 5, 7, 13); he *remembers* the words he receives (vv. 4, 6); he *embraces* the words of wisdom and makes them his own (v. 8); and he *obeys* them (v. 4). A student who never learns to honor and obey his superiors and "incline his ear to wisdom" will fail in other areas of character. According to the wise man of Proverbs, he will join the ranks of the fools and be destroyed (1:8–31). Those who struggle the hardest with character flaws are usually people who are unable to listen to counsel and heed good counsel. They never learned to honor their superiors. They failed the first grade in character and need to return and learn the hard lesson of honor and obedience.

Obedience is probably the most difficult lesson to teach. That's why we start on day one. It may require hundreds of lessons in a given day in the early years, and most parents will continue to teach it well into the teenage years. It is essential that the training come from a loving, caring parent or guardian. Above all, character education must be relationship based. (This principle is covered extensively in chapter 7.)

Signs of Life in Character Education

One trait that has marked the recent homeschooling movement is an emphasis on character. Today most state homeschool organizations sponsor annual conferences offering hundreds of workshops on a multitude of academic topics. Yet between 35 and 50 percent of the workshops at these conferences are focused on issues that one would think have little to do with academics—character development. In the past fifteen years, entire curriculum packages have been developed around character themes, such as the *Konos Unit Study* approach or Bill Gothard's *Advanced Training Institute* program. Supplemental resources are plentiful from programs such as *Doorposts, Pearables, and Focus on Character.* Character is seeing a comeback in education, especially as the free market exercises itself through the private school and homeschool movements.

Constructing the Building

If character is the foundation and framework of education, exactly how is this represented in the education of a child? Does one ignore geography, geometry, and geology in favor of character training? Absolutely not. However, one cannot consider the traditional academic fields and character development separately. To think that character is something taught for fifteen minutes during a special family time in the morning while the rest of the day is nothing but academics is to miss the picture. Character training must be taught *within* and *through* the academic subjects, with the focus always on the character of the child.

We had a child who was content to settle for a B grade in mathematics. It became very clear to us that it was not due to his ability, but because he was slothful. With another child we may have been content with a B grade, but for this child it was clearly a character issue. So we found that mathematics became the arena in which this child would learn conscientious diligence. Whenever this child missed enough problems to drop under 80 percent, he would have to repeat the entire series of lessons that preceded the test. The major purpose for this routine was not to improve his knowledge of mathematics; it was for training in character. Character is far more important than mathematics. If he skates through mathematics and never learns the character trait of diligence, then we have wallpaper without the wall. It turns out that mathematics is an opportunity to learn character. If the parent/teacher intentionally sets a priority on character, then he will carefully work these traits into the student *within* and *through* the academic courses of algebra, geography, composition, and history. If, however, a child grows up with a good comprehension of algebra but with incompetence in the lessons of Proverbs, the end result will be something less than a quality education.

Training character also requires a significant amount of involvement in the child's life. For any appreciable level of success there must be a huge investment of time, emotions, love, and two-way communication. Until a child is about twelve years old, there will be anywhere from twenty to two hundred separate opportunities to reinforce a character trait in any given day.

Practical Tips on Building Character

Is education broader than training, or is training broader than education? The overall preparation of a child is 95-percent character training, which should permeate the first twelve to eighteen developmental years. Character training is integrated into all learning. That's why it is impossible to distinguish between training and education. Although this book is not intended to consider all of the issues related to training, especially in the area of correcting bad behavior, here are several character building tips that every parent and teacher should consider.

1. Read at least five books that address the issue of training character. Be very wary about anything that is presented as "new." When it comes to training character, you simply cannot afford to ignore the age-old unassailable principles of the Bible. Whatever you do, *do not approach the training of a child without careful study of the following*

time-tested wisdom passages: Proverbs 10:13; 13:24; 22:15; 23:13–14; and 29:15.[2]

2. Always retain the humility to receive counsel or advice. Ask questions of those who have gone before.

3. Extensive early investment in training always pays a huge return. This is especially true with the lesson of obedience.

4. Very few lessons in life (especially in the area of character training) will be worth anything in the long run unless taught and reinforced with monotonous consistency. As far as it is humanly possible, every time a child clearly violates a rule, it must be addressed by the parent or mentor. Without consistency, problems will abound.

5. Expectations of the child should be communicated clearly to him or her. We write these expectations down and post them on the refrigerator. Expectations in the form of rules should be reasonable to the child's age and abilities. A good framework for rules is found in the Ten Commandments.

6. Watch for character deficiencies and modify teaching to accommodate these needs.

7. Do not minimize the importance or power of the Bible in addressing matters of the heart.

8. Never separate the lesson of faith from other character and behavior issues. Every child must face his basic problem of sinfulness, and he must be pointed to Christ if he is to enjoy the freedom of forgiveness.

9. Character is "Job One." It should be the number one consideration of any teacher/parent all day long, whether working in church, the geography class, the soccer field, the art class, the movie theater, or any other possible situation. Even during play times, children—

from infancy on—have opportunities to learn self-control. How is the child interacting with others? How is the child interacting with the material being studied? How is this experience assisting to develop this child's character?

10. Good character should be rewarded and commended as much as bad behavior is corrected.

Conclusion

Over the years I have worked with thousands of families in the area of education in state schools, private schools, and homeschools. In my experience, 95 percent of the cases in which families struggle with the education of a child, the primary issue is character. Yet that is the issue that tends to be relegated to the back burner. Too many parents are woefully ignorant in this area, and too many teachers seem to think that there is a dichotomy between packing facts into a student's brain and the development of character.

The priority of character in the *paideia* of a child was God's idea. World-famous for his wisdom, Solomon was the primary author of the book of Proverbs. According to 1 Kings 4:29–31 in the Bible, Solomon was blessed by God with this wisdom, such that he was "wiser than anyone." It is significant to note that his magnum opus was not a work in the area of nuclear physics. That is because the material was far more fundamental and significant than nuclear physics. The book of Proverbs is a book of character written for the training of the young student. You can count on this time-tested principle of education. It is impregnable to any "new" theories of education pitched by some twenty-first-century academic huckster. Something as important as educating children should never be left to the whims of modern fads that come and go. *The old paths, blazed by the Creator of children, will always be the safest.*

4 The Second Time-Tested Secret for a Successful Education:

Quality One-on-One Instruction

"Well Ben never took for granted
All his brother Billy's sacrifice.
Every night while the family slept
They would sit up late by that old lamp light,
Soundin' out the A's, and the E's,
and the I's and O's and U's.
Now he's readin' everything
from the cereal box to his Bible, three times through."[1]

The Second Time-Tested Secret for a Successful Education: Quality One-on-One Instruction

I could fill this chapter with stories of true heroes. These heroes date back to the beginning of time. The stories would tell about teachers, parents, brothers, and friends who invested themselves in the life of a child or adult. This investment of one-on-one mentorship accomplished far more than we could ever imagine in the development of the greatest thinkers, scientists, leaders, warriors, and parents the world has ever known. Most people can identify somebody in their lives who made an important investment of one-on-one time with them and helped make them the people they are today. Real progress in education and training will generally come one child at a time through the investment of time, energy, intellect, and emotion in one-on-one situations. Whether a child attends a conventional classroom or studies at the kitchen table, he will not progress without quality one-on-one instruction from parents, teachers, or friends.

Lessons from History

The modern classroom, where one teacher is assigned to twenty or thirty students, is a relatively new development in history. Although education reformists everywhere are crying out for smaller class sizes, class size is not the real issue. *The lack of consistent one-on-one instruction is the issue.* A first-grade teacher who works with a class of twenty-five students will not have more than six to seven minutes of one-on-one time with each student on any given day.

Throughout the ages the optimum form of education chosen by kings for their sons was the tutor. The tutor was hired for the purpose of providing the next monarch with the best education possible. While not everyone throughout history could afford this, there was no question that this would provide the best education.[2]

A brief survey of teaching situations in the Bible illustrates this methodology. From biblical example, it seems that one-on-one instruction is the regular form of instruction used in the education of children. While children were integrated into the congregation when public teaching occurred (see Deut. 4:10; Neh. 10:28; 12:43), children in the Bible typically learned in one-on-one situations. The method was almost always catechetical (by question and answer). What follows is a small sampling of educational situations described in this Book of God's wisdom.

> *When your children ask you, "What does this ritual mean to you?" you are to reply, "It is the Passover sacrifice to the LORD, for He passed over the houses of the Israelites in Egypt when He struck the Egyptians and spared our homes." Exodus 12:26–27*

In the future, when your son asks you, "What does this mean?" say to him, "By the strength of His hand the LORD brought us out of Egypt, out of the place of slavery."' Exodus 13:14

When your son asks you in the future, "What is the meaning of the decrees, statutes, and ordinances, which the LORD our God has commanded you?" tell him, "We were slaves of Pharaoh in Egypt, but the LORD brought us out of Egypt with a strong hand. Before our eyes the LORD inflicted great and devastating signs and wonders on Egypt, on Pharaoh and all his household, but He brought us from there." Deuteronomy 6:20–23

After three days, they found Him in the temple complex sitting among the teachers, listening to them and asking them questions. And all those who heard Him were astounded at His understanding and His answers.

Luke 2:46–47

So Jesus said to them, "When you lift up the Son of Man, then you will know that I am He, and that I do nothing on My own. But just as the Father taught Me, I say these things." John 8:28

Listen, my son, to your father's instruction, and don't reject your mother's teaching. Proverbs 1:8

A brief study of the teaching techniques of Jesus himself would find regular one-on-one contact. In fact, examples of one-on-one dialogue are replete throughout the Gospels. Jesus answered questions from Philip, Thomas, Judas, Peter, the woman at the well, Nicodemus, Nathanael, and others. At least sixty times we find Jesus engaged in some form of one-on-one discipleship with his disciples. In fact, one finds few sermons from Jesus in the Gospels and far more informal teaching situations.

Tutoring Works

The success of the tutorial method should be intuitively obvious. It is assumed in the ancient Book. Yet the method is easily lost in the modern industrial age where children are processed much like widgets in a manufacturing plant. It should not be surprising that studies on tutoring always evidence its superiority over the standard classroom method of teaching. One major study conducted in Great Britain with 2,372 elementary and junior high students, witnessed improvement in "reading comprehension 4.4 times the normal rate and word recognition 3.3 times the normal rate. Four months after the end of tutoring, the average tutee was still improving at twice the normal rate in both comprehension and word recognition."[3]

Another study found that "an after-school tutoring program in which low-achieving second- and third-graders were tutored for one hour twice each week by university students, retirees, and suburban mothers also generated strong improvements in the tutees' reading skills. Two reading specialists selected the children for tutoring, recruited and trained the tutors, and monitored the tutoring sessions. In each of two years, the tutored group outperformed a closely matched comparison group on word recognition, passage reading accuracy, and spelling. Fifty percent of the tutored children made a full year's gain in reading while only 20 percent of the comparison group children did."[4]

It should also be noted that the tutorial method is far more efficient for the individual student than the conventional classroom method. I like to consider education as a trip or an expedition. If a group of ten people set out on an expedition to a destination, there are different routes each can take to get from here to there. At any point, each person may be at a different location and on a slightly different route towards the destination. The reason the tutorial method is more efficient is that the tutor can apply himself directly to the specific route and the specific point the student visits as he moves along to his destination. It is also more efficient because the student can be better engaged by personal encounter. In my experience, the tutorial method of education takes about one third the time required by the conventional classroom approach to reach a particular goal. Research has found that home-educated students use only about one third to one half the time used in the classroom while producing academic results well beyond that achieved in the classroom.

When to Employ the Tutorial Approach

There are at least three major areas in which one-on-one instruction is necessary. First, one-on-one instruction is best applied when new material is first introduced to a child. For the most part, teaching children to read in a one-on-thirty format is an exercise in futility. This is because reading introduces an abstract concept to a child. Teaching a child that black scratches on a white page actually mean something introduces a radical concept to a child's mind. This is one of the reasons why the best educators today encourage parents to teach their children to read *before* they send them to first grade. Of course, this may not work for every child because not every child is ready to read at six years of age. But assuming that a child is ready to read, in most cases it will take twenty minutes of one-on-one time, five days a week for a year to teach that child to read. An initial investment of quality one-on-one instruction every day for a year will pay back in great measure because good reading has always been essential for learning. (This idea will be better developed in chapter 8.)

Mathematics is another subject requiring a great deal of one-on-one time. Again, this is essential for the first year or two as the subject is introduced and the children begin to grasp the concepts of numbers, addition, subtraction, multiplication, and division. With the introduction of each new concept, some one-on-one time is needed. The more basic the new concept introduced, the more essential is the one-on-one investment.

Why is it that children cannot learn new conceptual material effectively in a *lecture?* The reason for this is found in the principle of individuality (see chapter 6). I believe much of this is tied to the nature of the brain. When a child is young, he has relatively few connections in his mind to which he can tie the new material. Therefore it is essential that a teacher knows something about those connections that do exist. Connections will always be different for each child; but similarities will exist, especially for those who are part of the same family or who share a fairly homogenous cultural background. Additionally, each child learns at a different rate and requires repetition either in the form of verbal reminders or exercises in different areas.

Second, one-on-one instruction is valuable when a student is struggling. In my years of teaching, I have found that I can lecture on a subject and try to address all of the common problem areas in the lecture. Yet inevitably, upon putting forward the assignment, twenty hands go up in the air, and each student has a different question or needs help over a different impediment. So, in the course of a student's study, he may find himself getting "stuck" in a certain area. Unless a tutor is there at the specific point at which he needs help, frustration will set in. Either the student will ignore the problem and move on, to his own detriment, or he will quit.

Third, one-on-one situations are necessary when we are teaching major life lessons, especially in the area of character. Most of the book of Proverbs operates in the area of character and faith. Almost every chapter or section of the book is introduced with the address, "My son." The method exemplified in Proverbs is one-on-one teaching. It is the father and mother individually guiding their son in the ways of Yahweh. This one-on-one training is crucial to developing self-discipline in a child. In the early years, a child will not be able to discipline himself to do things that require effort and push his own comfort zone. A mentor who properly understands the child and his potential must motivate by positive or negative reinforcement to train those character traits of diligence, patience, and courage into that child.

The goal in education is to see increasing levels of independence in the student as he learns how to learn. This means that maximum one-on-one time will be necessary for the first seven to eight years of a child's life. *Every parent ought to see that their children get at least one hour a day of one-on-one instruction for at least two full academic years in the early part of their academic development.* This is a bare minimum to assure good academic progress. Some children will require more, but very few children will require less than this. This one-on-one time should steadily decrease over time. In general, by the time a child is thirteen years old, he should be able to study independently for most of the day. If this is not happening, it is usually because there was not adequate one-on-one time spent in the early years. Older students should be encouraged to strive for independence in problem solving. An important part of one-on-one tutoring is to avoid giving the answer to a question if a student can be shown *how* to find the answer himself. This can be done by asking him leading questions or directing him to certain tools or resources.

Quality One-on-One Teaching

What follows is a list of helpful suggestions for maximizing one-on-one encounters in teaching situations.

1. Use the catechetical device. Asking the right questions will flesh out where your student is in reference to the material at hand. Encourage the student to ask questions also. The free flow of questions and answers is the best way to get to the heart and the mind of your child. By the way, this is the essential core of the ancient Hebraic method of education, recovered in the passages listed at the beginning of this chapter. Ironically, some modern academicians are *rediscovering* the power of dialogue in the formation of a quality

education. For instance, Dr. Jane Healy states: "In those precious times together at the dinner table, for example, parents who take the time to discuss topics thoughtfully, who talk about events and ideas, are helping their children become much better thinkers than those who focus more on the food or the situation at hand."[5] Dr. Healy cites studies indicating "'frequent responsive mother-child language interaction' was the most critical factor in raising mental ability. . . . A child's early experiences with language have powerful long-term effects on school achievement."[6]

2. Always explain a concept in words and illustrations that you know are familiar to the student. If you cannot do this, one of two problems exist. Either you do not understand the material yourself, or you do not know the child, his experiences, his background, his culture, or his language. Your relationship with the student is not what it should be. (More on this in chapter 7.)

3. When explaining a particularly difficult concept to a student, try several different methods, and then hone in on the method that works the best.

4. Make sure the student is fully engaged. This is where the one-on-one method excels, so make full use of it. Eye contact, touch (where appropriate), and calling the student by name are powerful ways to accomplish this.

5. When you are introducing a new concept for the first time, be sure that you are well-prepared and you have sufficient time to provide the best introduction possible. Explain the concept *carefully and correctly*. Fresh material hits the brain like a footprint on fast-drying concrete. Get it right the first time.

6. Make full use of motivating language, affirmation, and genuine enthusiasm. Engage the student's emotions and will, as well as his mind, on the subject.

7. Do not give away the answer in every case, especially if you think the student can get the answer himself. Lead him to it by a series of questions or by pointing him in the right direction.

8. If you do give an answer away, make sure the student works on similar problems himself. Then recheck his work for accuracy. This will ascertain that the child is ready to proceed down the route on his expedition.

9. Work into yourself the character traits of a good tutor. These include perceptive ears and eyes, patience, gentleness, and love.

10. Send in the reserve tutor! There are times when one parent or one teacher simply cannot find the right method to get a child through a difficult piece of the academic journey. When my wife comes to the end of the rope as she works with one of our children in some academic challenge, I jump into the mix. Usually, I can resolve the problem in short order. The difference is not a matter of brains or even credentials. Another person who is already well acquainted with that child simply brings to the one-on-one situation *another perspective*. Two perspectives are better than one.

Conclusion

The literacy problem in this country has reached epidemic proportions, and much of this is due to a lack of good tutorial programs, especially in the early years of a child's academic development. The many reading programs (and phonics programs) marketed to families lately through the media, the department stores, and within the home education movement should bear witness to the success of this particular method of one-on-one instruction.

The present-day establishment has trained us to think that education is very complicated, only suited to the hands of certified professionals. This is far from the truth. Actually, education is rooted far deeper in relationships than in intellect or in a technical formula. Recent studies have shown that peer-based tutoring works better than an adult tutoring the child. This is because children today are closer to their peers. They relate better to their peers because they share common experiences, language, and culture. As we will discover in chapter 7, the key is relationships.

5 The Third Time-Tested Secret for a Successful Education:

The Principle of Protection

I was raised on an island. In 1969, my father had decided to take his family to the mission field in Japan. He planted churches, wrote and published books, and evangelized the southern island of Kyushu, all the while homeschooling his six children with the faithful assistance of my mother. Thirty years later, as my father visited with my family in Denver, Colorado, we reminisced together about those early years in Japan. I asked him why he decided to go to Japan as a missionary and his answer surprised me. He said he wanted to take the gospel to Japan, but it was more than that. Before leaving for Japan, he had taught in American public schools in the 1950s, and then in private, Christian schools in the 1960s. After those experiences he decided *he did not want to raise his children in this culture*. So he set out to make his own culture for his family on an island out in the Pacific Ocean.

Though many families have been shamed for "sheltering" their children, we would have been considered the sheltered poster children of the 1960s and 1970s. By the time I graduated from high school, I knew *no one* who had a raising quite like ours. Even those who recognize some value in sheltering would have thought my parents had overdone it. Books in the house were scoured and edited, sometimes with black markers. The only American movie I remember watching during my teenage years was *The Sound of Music*. But somewhere around the semi-romantic scene, "I am 16, going on 17," the television went off, and we were all sent off to bed.

Returning stateside in 1981, I enrolled in a prominent West Coast public university majoring in mechanical engineering. My parents returned to the mission field and I was on my own. After several years at the university, this strange sheltered boy, raised on an island out in the middle of the Pacific Ocean, was elected student body president at a university of seventeen thousand students. I ran an exceedingly competitive campaign against five other candidates. It took three elections and hundreds of speeches and debates, but in the end I emerged the winner.

I have reflected on this unusual upbringing and the immediate success I enjoyed following those early years. I look at the six children produced in that environment. All went on to obtain college degrees, and four achieved graduate degrees. All have a clear sense of purpose in life, and all fulfill a part of the vision our parents had for us — serving God in some capacity somewhere around the world.

Looking back at this apparent paradox, I have repeatedly asked the question: What happened? How could so much sheltering produce such balance? It is true that the principle of protection is ineffective of itself. If a child is put in a closet for eighteen years, he *will* be maladjusted to real life. Protection is insufficient by itself. Yet as my parents provided us with a highly unusual degree of protection, their over-riding operational purpose was *preparation*. While they set up an umbrella of protection over their six children on the island, they were actively preparing us to make a significant impact on the world.

The Third Time-Tested Secret for a Successful Education: The Principle of Protection

But whoever causes the downfall of one of these little ones who believe in Me — it would be better for him if a heavy millstone were hung around his neck and he were drowned in the depths of the sea! Matthew 18:6

This verse could very well be the most frightening verse in the Bible. Such grim words coming from the lips of Jesus should cause any parent or teacher to stop for a moment and ponder. Children are important to Jesus. Words couched in such a severe warning should stand out like a lighted neon sign to any parent or teacher skimming the book of Matthew. Note also what it is that would merit the millstone treatment — placing an occasion to stumble in the path of a child. This timeless truth teaches that children must be protected from hindrances while they are shepherded down the pathway of wisdom.

Periodically someone will justify a seeming lack of protectiveness by telling me that their children are being missionaries to the world. Is this really what God calls seven-year-old children to do? Should we pack their bags and send them off to cannibals in the jungles of New Guinea to preach the gospel? It should be obvious that children are not ready to go into the jungles until they have received adequate preparation.

I previously defined *education* as the preparation of a child physically, intellectually, emotionally, and spiritually for life and eternity. For a child to be prepared in all aspects of his being, he ought to be *protected* — physically, intellectually, emotionally, and spiritually — while that is happening. A seven-year-old child is physically unprepared to take on missionary work in the jungles. He is emotionally a bit unfit for the job as well. His intellect may still be a little underdeveloped, and he may not be able to present a well-constructed defense of his faith. Spiritually, he may not be up to facing the challenges that might come his way from the natives with bones through their noses and navels.

The purpose of education is preparation. Children are not called to be missionaries at seven, eight, or nine years of age. Neither should they be sent to school to be a missionary there. They should not be sent to school to teach others, but to be taught.

Difficult though it may be to imagine or accept, there are forces in this world that *really* hurt children. These influences can bring about physical, emotional, intellectual, or spiritual ruin. Though this is true for children and adults, it is children who are more vulnerable to lifelong damage from such adverse circumstances.

The Principles of Protection

The principle of protection must be taken into account in the education of a child. Though it is possible to misapply this principle, I suggest this is not the case with most children today. On the contrary, many families suffer from the total disregard of this vital factor. Yet the principle must be carefully studied by every parent of every child for each situation in which the children find themselves. Individual families should make fitting applications of the principle of protection; however, there are a few universal rules that should be considered as this principle is employed:

1. No one is ever completely immune to the damage caused by unsavory influences. There is always a role for some accountability and watchfulness on the part of every man and woman on the face of the earth. That protection may include self-denial and self-discipline, but it also includes an accountability to friends and brothers.

2. The degree of protection required by a child will decrease over time as the child becomes increasingly grounded in the truth, stabilizes emotionally, and grows stronger both physically and spiritually. For example, a two-year-old cannot handle the emotional abuse

that a twenty-year-old could bear. A seven-year-old child may not react correctly to peers mocking her on the playground, whereas a sixteen-year-old should be ready to take it in stride.

3. Every child is an individual, and therefore some will require more protection than others. "Our sister is young; she has no breasts. What will we do for our sister on the day she is spoken for? If she is a wall, we will build a silver parapet on it. If she is a door, we will enclose it with cedar planks" (Song of Songs 8:8–9). The difference between the two children here depicted is the character trait of "impressionableness." One twelve-year-old girl is characterized as a door and must be protected by boards of cedar. She is vulnerable and impressionable. The other, who is depicted as a wall, guards herself and needs much less outside protection.

The Extent of Protection

Somehow a parent/mentor must be able to gauge the level of protection necessary for each child. This must begin with a realistic understanding of the dangers involved. There is a world out there that stands in opposition to our morals, our faith, or even our persons. There are opposing worldviews that dot the academic and cultural landscapes. Not all worldviews are of equal merit; neither do they agree on the most fundamental propositions of all (more on this in chapter 11). A child must be protected from opposing worldviews and from falsehood, especially in the early years.

But how do we determine how much protection to require for our children? How much protection is too much protection? The following wisdom passage provides a helpful standard to answer this all-important question:

Since the weapons of our warfare are not fleshly, but are powerful through God for the demolition of strongholds. We demolish arguments and every high-minded thing that is raised up against the knowledge of God, taking

every thought captive to the obedience of Christ. And we are ready to punish
any disobedience, once your obedience is complete. 2 Corinthians 10:4–6

The acid test determining whether a child is ready to be subjected to an environment hostile to his own worldview and faith is found here: the child must be prepared to confront the world, to wrestle with principalities and powers, to cast down imaginations that oppose the knowledge of God, and to bring into captivity every thought to the obedience of Christ. It is a tall order indeed, for there are many forms of imaginations out there. If a child is not prepared to cast down the imaginations of a naturalist philosophy, he simply should not be subjected to the bombardment of naturalism. If he is not prepared to cast down the imaginations of egalitarianism, God-eliminating evolution, materialist socialism, relativism, environmentalism, atheism, pluralism, or sexual "freedom," then he should not be subjected to a steady diet of it. Many children cannot even define these terms, let alone discern them or cast them down. Yet these philosophies are expressed every day in classrooms and media programs through textbooks, music, television, movies, the Internet, and discussions.

An important part of education is to prepare children to grapple with the antithesis, with that which opposes what they believe. This usually takes place in the junior and senior high years of development (sometimes called the critical and rhetoric stages of learning).

As children develop, the preparation given them should allow for the removal of layers of protection. Their preparation must include at least the following elements:

1. *Truth.* They must be firmly planted on the principles of truth. These truths become a matter of conviction in their hearts and lives. They should be able to stand for the truth against opposition.

2. *Self-awareness.* They must be well aware of their own areas of weakness in order to provide protection for themselves.

3. *Testing.* They should be subjected to certain tests under supervision of the parent/teacher. Initially the tests should be obvious tests between what is right and wrong, true and false (avoiding the deceptive and ambiguous). If they respond correctly, then there is evidence that they can stand under more difficult opposition. The tests given will challenge them emotionally, intellectually, and spiritually. These tests should be done in close connection with the mentor. This provides opportunities for follow-up discussions.

It would be unwise to take a child out of a warm, protective home and abruptly place him into an antagonistic environment for seven hours a day without some training as to how to operate in that environment. With a few rare exceptions, such abrupt transitions do not work well. There is the story of the fellow who explained how his father taught him to swim: "It was in the old-fashioned way," he said. "He took me out into the middle of the lake and threw me in. Swimming to shore wasn't bad. It was getting out of the gunny sack that took a little work."

Proper Protection

To properly protect a child from certain influences that could corrupt the training and trip the child, you must take the following steps:

1. *Monitor the inputs.* Almost no one today lives in isolated, rural farming communities. Young people in small towns are just as susceptible to drug addiction, criminal activity, or unedifying music and media as are those who live in larger towns. Your children may not have access to harmful influences because of certain rules you have imposed in your home, but you should count on the fact that their peers do have that access. Parents must be engaged in their children's lives enough to know what is coming into their eyes and ears (and hearts and minds) via peers or television programs. Unmonitored

television and movie watching will very likely be problematic and potentially counterproductive to the education and training that they are receiving. While a whole chapter should be dedicated to the topic of peer relationships, the book of Proverbs is packed with warnings and admonitions such as: "The one who walks with the wise will become wise, but a companion of fools will suffer harm" (Prov. 13:20). Parents must know about their children's associations. Who are their friends? What backgrounds do they bring into the association? What is the nature of that relationship? How does that relationship affect the child? The parent or mentor must be aware of the other influences (or inputs) in the child's life. This awareness is essential for proper discipleship, to properly address these influences in the teaching program, or to modify them if they become counterproductive to the overall *paideia* (education) program.

2. *Control the inputs.* Though very necessary, this is the most difficult and sometimes the most painful part of the education and training of a child. Anyone who thinks that a seven-year-old child can properly resist and address the deceptive and immoral ideas that an intellectually, emotionally, and spiritually mature forty-five-year-old man can handle has simply lost contact with reality.

The fact is, parents/mentors should control the *amount of time* in which children receive inputs that could produce adverse effects. One of the sharpest differences between home-educated children and others is found in the time spent watching television. The major study previously mentioned, conducted by Dr. Rudner, found that homeschooled children spent only a quarter of the time the average child in America spends watching television. Television can be mind-sapping. At the very least, it can turn into a pitiful waste of time. It does not stimulate the mind to critical analysis and "filling in the pieces." It *leads* the mind but does not *challenge* it.

I suggest that one of the most straightforward and simple things you can do to guarantee a great education for your children is to control the television. Some families may find this difficult. In such cases, television should be eliminated altogether. We permit our children to watch television or videos once a week. Anything beyond that seems to lead to slothful dependency on television for our family.

After several years of setting limits on television, we found that our children have come to prefer reading over television. Routinely we give our children the choice of watching a television program or hearing a great story read out loud. They choose the latter. If you control television *to some extent,* children will usually turn to reading. In most cases, this change in habit and taste comes about within just a few years. And almost inevitably, you will find them scoring between the 80th and 90th percentile in reading on standardized tests. In the rare instance when a child does not turn to reading, chances are he will be digging up gophers in the backyard and skinning them for pelts, which arguably is more productive than watching television.

Controlling television may also involve limiting the time children spend in the homes of others. The technological age has produced a few more challenges to a child's development. Video games and the Internet can stymie a child's moral, spiritual, or intellectual growth. The same dangers inherent to the television apply to these new technologies.

Controlling the inputs involves positioning the student in an environment that is healthy for him. He should have access to regular oversight and mentoring, especially from parents. The books to which he has access at home, church, school, or the public library ought to be those that best nurture him spiritually, emotionally, and intellectually. Most books written for children in our day are nothing more than cotton candy for the brain. If children learn to enjoy cotton candy, they will tend to shy away from vegetables and prime rib. If all the books that hold up your bookshelves are "cotton candy," then that is what your children will learn to enjoy. Parents who feed their children cotton candy for breakfast, lunch, and dinner will not see their children thrive physically. Parents who stock their bookshelves with "cotton candy" for the brain, will not see their children thrive in other ways. It is also wise to restrict access to books that *promote* immoral behavior, such as disrespect for parents, obscene and blasphemous language, improper sexual behavior, witchcraft, and the like (see Phil. 4:8). Also, avoid books that repeat overly simplistic and predictable plots *ad nauseam*. Find books that describe complex characters, present good triumphing over evil, commend the character traits of Proverbs, and books that actually teach something about the world (such as history, geography, and the nature of the men and animals that populate the world). As a child's tastes mature, you should be able to provide him with more liberty to make his own choices in his reading.

Controlling peer associations is a matter of planning and controlling the child's extracurricular time. Certain peer associations may be acceptable for limited periods of time. You will also find that great amounts of unmonitored play time spent between certain children can become counterproductive to your training and education efforts. Foolishness is bound in the heart of children (Prov. 22:15), and the foolishness of children out from under the careful eye and patient guidance of a mentor tends to multiply exponentially. You may need to monitor some associations closer than others.

Wisdom Tips

There are several wisdom tips the parent/mentor should keep in mind before setting out to control the inputs.

1. Removing something is much harder than not providing it in the first place. Take great care when choosing a church, a neighborhood, or a school (whether he will attend the school full-time or part-time). Be especially careful about associations through youth groups and clubs. Realize that if your children are going to spend any concerted time with certain friends, they will start to act, think, and look like

those friends. Before bringing your children into these associations, take a look at the group and ask yourself the question, "Do I want my child to look like these children in his character and conduct?" If you exercise great caution before committing to any associations, it is less likely you will have to remove the child from that group later.

2. Removing a negative influence without replacing it is an exercise in futility. Children who wander into close association with what Proverbs calls "the mocker" (Prov. 13:1; 22:10; see also Ps. 1:1), learn to *prefer* these associations. Removing these associations is difficult but not impossible. The challenge here for both the parent/mentor and the child is to utilize the motivation, creativity, wisdom, discipline, and patient love needed to find new associations, new activities, and new entertainment. This will also require retraining the child's tastes for something better. Any parent or mentor who denies the young student access to certain entertainment or associations should provide something else in its place. For example, parents who deny their children access to cheap and unedifying thrills could present exciting alternatives such as a family missionary trip to the Amazon jungle or building a house for a needy widow in the neighborhood.

3. The singular importance of character training is once more underscored. None of the advice presented here will work without respect for authority. If children never learn to respect the wisdom and guidance of their teachers, it is doubtful they will appreciate the wisdom of protection. Moreover, the lesson of contentment and gratitude is crucial. There is hardly a child alive who doesn't prefer the grass on the other side of the fence. The only cure for this is to learn to "count your blessings."

4. Everything we have discussed here is rooted in a relationship. Without a heart-deep relationship between the father and the son, the mentor and the student, chances are the young person will seek out another crowd for his values and direction in life. We will discuss this aspect more in chapter 7.

No Monolithic Set of Rules

Notice that I have not suggested any set standard for every family. In fact, I have consciously avoided recommending particular curriculum, books, movies, or recreations. The standards that a family lays down will depend greatly on their understanding of what constitutes good character and good education. We have already addressed this in principle, but each family must define in more precise terms its own vision and goals in their children's education. Moreover, the strengths and weaknesses that reside in individual families are important considerations in constructing proper shelters for each home.

The Purpose of Protection

At this point, a word of caution is in order. The principle of protection can easily be misunderstood and misapplied. This happens when protection becomes an end in itself. Indeed, the world that opposes what is true and what is right may be a dangerous place, but that does not mean we are to fear it. In my estimation there are three possible relationships a person may have with a world antagonistic to his own belief system. First, he may escape that world. As a pure option, this is ultimately unreasonable and impossible. After all, he will have to go out to shop for groceries from time to time. Second, he may *amalgamate* into that world and become like it. The Bible wisely warns against this by telling us not to conform to the world (Rom. 12:1–2). Third, the individual may change the world. This is the calling that Jesus places on all of us. We do not hide the light under a bushel. We set it on a candlestick so as to light the surroundings and impact the world around us (Matt. 5:13–16). The goal of protection is preparation.

Conclusion

We began this chapter with a shocking warning from Jesus himself: whatever you do, protect your children from harmful influences. This basic principle for the education of a child is a primary concern for parents. It is a rare parent who wants to ruin his children. After all, no one seeks the best interests of a child more than that child's own parents. In addition, no one knows a child's weaknesses and strengths better than that child's parents. A child's education, entertainment, and associations are all under the authority of parents. Yet parents need to be reminded that they are in control. Many parents today delegate the oversight of children to others without carefully considering the new set of influences that could enter their children's lives. It is tempting to think that if we bring professionals into the raising of our children, we are relieved of any responsibility for the results that follow. But that is a false pretense. For it is the parent (not professionals) that will suffer the consequences if we fail to carefully monitor our children and the inputs that influence them. More often than not, we are led to think that professionals should be implicitly trusted, as if they will be as caring and as discerning as parents. This is a fatal assumption. Truth, nature, and history defy any such supposition. In fact, this is the point at which our parenting and our social institutions begin to unravel. When parents understand their position and their responsibility in relation to their child's development and education, they will begin to make conscious and careful choices concerning an education program—choices that *must* take into account the prime principle of protection.

The Fourth Time-Tested Secret for a Successful Education:
The Principle of Individuality

When my wife and I were young parents, we set out to arrange the best possible education for our first child. We lined our bookshelves with popular books that encouraged us to start academics as early as possible if we were going to nurture a young prodigy. As time went on, however, other books informed us that the real problem with the modern education systems was that they introduce students to academic rigors *too early*. We were confused. We soon realized that most of these books made universal statements and established principles that were neither time-tested nor absolute. While the ideas conveyed may have been helpful to some, they would be hurtful to others. These popular authors made the fatal mistake of ignoring the principle of individuality.

Two seconds after our second child emerged from the womb, we learned something about children. We said what all parents say in the delivery room on the birth of their second child: "They are so *different!*" By the time our third child came along, we didn't bother saying it. After all, there's no sense in repeating the obvious! Some children are unbelievably different, and others are shockingly different. It would be comical, if it were not so tragic, that the most obvious fact of parenting is the most ignored principle in modern education systems.

The Fourth Time-Tested Secret for a Successful Education: The Principle of Individuality

A common educational methodology used in both private schools and homeschools throughout the country since it was developed in the 1960s is known as the "Principle Approach." The first premise taught in this system is known as the "The Principle of Individuality." It is framed in a simple child's verse taken from the book *Teaching and Learning America's Christian History* by Rosalie Slater:

> *God made me special like no one else you see,*
>
> *A testimony to his diversity.[1]*

Every child is an individual, endowed with special and unique gifts, talents, and abilities by his Creator. No two persons on Earth share the same DNA. In a sampling of one thousand persons, no two will look alike, act alike, or think alike. Of all of the common-sense facts accessible to men, this one should be among the most obvious.

Unfortunately, this fact has been largely ignored in the development of school-based education in the Western world. In fact, the educational mantra that has resounded repeatedly throughout the past 150 years—from politicians and academics alike—has been "standardize" and "centralize." In the late 1800s it was common for small groups of children, aged eight to sixteen, to gather in a one-room schoolhouse a mile down the road as one teacher worked with them. Over time, school districts began to establish themselves and centralize control of these individual schools under one head or board. Eventually departments of education centralized control on the state level, developing and standardizing methodologies and curriculum. Experts were hired to establish those methodologies for every child in the state. By the 1970s and 1980s, both major political parties supported the establishment and expansion of a United States Department of Education. The belief was that wise experts could establish standardized goals, standardized tests, and standardized methodologies for every child in the country—from the Native American communities of southwest Colorado, to the inner-city children of Chicago, to the suburban children of Atlanta, to the Hispanic children of Southern California. Standardized goals and curriculum could now be set for 150 million children—children with 150 million different sets of talents, gifts, and learning styles, coming from 150 million unique backgrounds.

In today's age of materialism and naturalism, the child is treated less and less as a personal soul and more like a chemical process. In our industrial age of high-volume manufacturing, education takes on similar mechanistic processes. Children, however, cannot be processed as widgets are processed in a manufacturing plant. In manufacturing, raw material is introduced to a standardized process in order to produce a high-quality product with as little variation as possible. The important thing to recognize in manufacturing is that the raw material introduced to the process must be exactly the same— the same basic raw material with uniform dimensions. If what goes into the process has very little variation, then what comes out will have very little variation, resulting in a consistent quality product.

The problem is that children are not widgets. You simply cannot force all children into a single process and expect the end result to be a "quality product." Children come in all shapes and sizes, with a wide variety of genetic and family backgrounds, not to mention thinking methods, learning styles, intellectual abilities, and growth patterns.

Still, education has become organized under a set of one-size-fits-all standards. Classroom teachers, school districts, state departments of education, and textbook manufacturers maintain a standard of expectations for every student in the class. The ubiquitous number above the classroom door hangs over the head of every child entering. The grade level on the spine of the book shouts out what every child is expected to achieve in the fourth grade or the fifth grade. The standard is set, and it is the same for every child in the classroom.

When subjected to this standard, however, roughly half the class will be intimidated by the material while the other half of the class will be bored. A few in the middle may be well suited to the material. Or a student may do well in the class for one year, but slow down or accelerate the next academic year. The problem gets worse. A student who does well in math does not always do well in the language class down the hall. Each student has a different set of God-given aptitudes and abilities. When all students are subjected to the same standards, the same program, the same method of curriculum, the same level of curriculum, and the same teaching methods, the end result will resemble the disastrous consequence of square pegs (or triangular pegs) jammed into round holes. The results of an educational methodology based in a flawed anthropology are nothing less than tragic. The high-volume, standardized approach may be effective in manufacturing widgets and may appear to *be efficient* in highly centralized forms of education, but in the end it is not *effective* in education because children are not widgets.

This monolithic tower is a surprisingly recent development in education. An eighteenth-century Patrick Henry roamed the streams and woods with his flintlock when he should have been in the fourth grade. In his teenage years, his father gave him five years of Latin, Greek, math, and history, and Patrick Henry became the greatest orator this country ever knew. There were no grade levels and no standards. Each young person had his own life, his own calling, and his own unique preparation for life. Patrick took the goal of his education from his clergyman uncle, which was "not to covet other men's goods; but to learn and labor truly to get *my* own living, and to do my duty in that state of life unto which it shall please God to call me."[2]

The nation that grew to be the world power of the twentieth century was built on one-room schoolhouses without standards. Barely one hundred years ago, Laura Ingalls Wilder entered her first classroom as a teacher and quickly assessed the progress of her five students. She writes about a little nine-year-old, Ruby, who "had finished the First Reader, and in arithmetic she was learning subtraction. . . . The little boy was eleven, and had finished the Second Reader, and reached short division. . . . Clarence, Charles, and Martha were all in the Fourth Reader. . . . None of them had studied grammar or history, but Martha had brought her mother's grammar book and Clarence had a history book."[3]

My wife and I have five students in our one-room schoolhouse out on the eastern plains of Colorado. When my children are asked their grade levels, they usually respond with their age. My twelve-year-old son is studying second-year algebra, ninth-grade vocabulary and spelling, eighth-grade reading, and seventh-grade grammar. My ten-year-old daughter is studying eighth-grade vocabulary, ninth-grade reading, and fifth-grade math. We have always ignored the grade levels on the spines of the books they use, except to determine the sequence of study. Three-time New York Teacher-of-the-Year John Taylor Gatto comments on his own philosophy of education and frustration with the modern boxed system: "David learns to read at age four; Rachel, at age nine. In normal development, when both are 13, you can't tell which one learned first—the five-year spread means nothing at all. But in school I label Rachel 'learning disabled' and slow David down a bit, too. For a paycheck, I adjust David to depend on me to tell him to go and stop. He won't outgrow that dependency. I identify Rachel as discount merchandise, 'special education' fodder. She'll be locked in her place forever."[4] Grade levels are relatively new, artificial constructions intended to help institutions run more efficiently. They *do not,* however, ensure that students are mastering knowledge and understanding in the classroom.

Children who have been pressed into the classic one-size-fits-all educational system for a long time eventually become resistant and frustrated with education. After years of falling off the wagon of reading or math and being dragged under the wheels, they become jaded with the whole academic scene. If they do not happen to fit into the classroom standard set for every class and in every grade, they are destined for an education in frustration, a crisis of self-confidence, and unnecessary emotional and intellectual struggles in their critical developing years.

The principle of individuality is the most *liberating* principle of all the time-tested principles. It can be wielded with amazing adaptability and powerful effectiveness in the home. In almost every case in which a parent removes a struggling child from the monolithic system into the one-room schoolhouse of the home, the principle of individuality is invoked. The principle removes a tremendous amount of pressure from the backs of children and parents alike.

I further suggest that from the perspective of purely intellectual or academic performance, this principle is the most *powerful* principle of all. That is because this principle takes the individual gifts and abilities of a child and maximizes them! It does not waste time grinding square pegs into round holes. It recognizes differences in children and allows for those differences. A child may be two years behind in one particular subject at one particular point in his academic journey, but a parent-teacher who recognizes this powerful principle will wisely, courageously, and patiently adapt the material to the student's capabilities. The mentor challenges the student at his strong points while simultaneously affirming whatever progress is made on the weaker points. The goal is to maximize the child's potential at every point in the journey. The child is never discouraged that he is behind another child in one particular area. The mentor carefully avoids comparing the child with others. Those who have had the standardized system ingrained in them know how easy it is to say to a child, "Why aren't you in fifth-grade math yet? What's wrong with you? Your brother was well ahead of you at this age!" Academic competition may come into play at points but usually in the area of the child's strengths. The program for each child ought to be such that the child is reminded that he is an individual. He is praised and affirmed for doing his best as he makes good use of his God-given talents and abilities.

The principle of individuality is applied in two different ways in the area of education.

1. It is manifested in the *rate* of comprehension. No two children learn at precisely the same rate. They certainly do not learn all subjects at the same rate. Now it is much more difficult to practice this principle than to teach it. I had taught it for years before my seven-year-old daughter began struggling with math. This was a crushing blow to me because math has always been my forté and my love. Imagine the trauma I felt when my daughter could not absorb her addition tables! For six months she worked on her tables, and she was falling behind. My wife reminded me of everything I had been teaching for years about the principle of individuality, so eventually I resigned myself to the fact that Emily would never be a math whiz. So as she slipped a year "behind," I came to peace with the fact that Emily would always be a little behind in math. But we continued to encourage and affirm her painfully slow progress in math. Then one day, something happened. She comprehended. Something had clicked. Perhaps her mind had developed in a key area. We may have explained some key concept in such a way that she could understand. Today Emily is at least a year ahead of the average performance for her age level in mathematics.

I was not so naive as to believe that everyone advances at the same rate of comprehension as this:

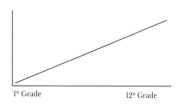

1ˢᵗ Grade   12ᵗʰ Grade

But for some reason, I thought everyone advanced at different linear rates as the following diagram illustrates:

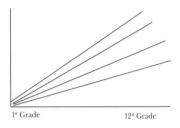

As it turns out, however, rates of comprehension are far less linear, much like the diagram below:

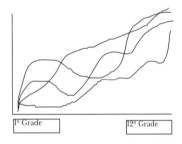

Try to standardize that! These remarkably nonlinear learning patterns are the reason why children cannot be processed through our schools by the same method, maintaining the same expectations, and at the same rate of instruction. Imagine the difficulty of putting a standardized program together to meet that pattern!

2. The principle of individuality is also manifested in the *manner* of comprehension, also known as learning style. There are many approaches to this area of study, just as there are many different ways to cut a cake. The most popular way to break down learning styles is by means of sensory learning methods: auditory, visual, and kinesthetic. The auditory learner learns best by means of hearing. The visual learner learns best by means of sight. The kinesthetic learner learns best by feel and action. Most children use a mix of

learning styles and eventually learn to accommodate other learning methods.

Learning styles are far more complex and varied than the simple sensory divisions. In fact, there are thousands of ways to explain just about anything. There are thousands of learning methods. Therefore, a parent-teacher must learn something about his student in order to meet that student's particular learning apparatus. In many cases, it would be impossible for the teacher to explain *how* he taught a particular lesson to a particular student. Much of teaching works in the intangible realm because it is based on what the teacher has learned about the student. While it is sometimes helpful to recognize a particular learning style, much more time should be spent studying the student than studying books on learning styles!

Several years ago I attended a convention on excellence in teaching sponsored by the governor of the state. The seminar was conducted by a professor from a university in Tennessee. The entire day was taken up with extolling the virtues of standardized testing. Halfway through the afternoon, someone asked the expert what exactly it contributed to the success of some teachers. It was the question for which we had all been waiting. His answer came as no surprise to me: "It's flexibility," he told the crowd of five hundred teachers and administrators. "The teachers who are flexible, adapting their methods and curriculum to each student in the classroom, are the most successful." The expert continued, "There is a problem, however. These studies show that a child who receives one of these better teachers will *not* exhibit sustained improvement unless he has that excellent teacher *for three years in a row*." No solutions were proposed in that particular conference.

Why would it take at least three years of one good teacher investing in a student before any lasting return is seen on the investment? Could it be that it would require at least that many years for the teacher to know the student? A good teacher-student relationship is essential before any fruitful education can progress. Where would you find this kind of relationship?

Where would you find a long-term, nurturing and caring relationship for a child? Who knows a child better than anyone else? The obvious answer is the parent. Major studies conducted on home education over the last fifteen years have shown repeatedly that there is zero statistical difference between the academic performance of children taught by parents who are teacher-certified and the performance of children taught by parents who are not teacher-certified. Please understand, these findings do not necessarily mean that teacher certification and all of the educational preparation associated with it are entirely without value (especially with respect to institutional schooling). But, there is a principle that transcends all other principles in education, a dominating factor that washes out all other factors that purport to contribute to success in the education of a child: it is this factor of individuality and the concomitant principle of relationship-based education (which will be covered in greater detail in the next chapter).

The Origin of the Principle

The principle of individuality should be obvious to any parent with more than one child. For some reason, however, it is forgotten when the child reaches six years of age. It is a mystery that this factor is of little concern to the educational experts and bureaucrats of our day. A driving factor in modern education theory is the desire to see all children receiving the same "high-quality" education. The intentions are admirable. The effects of their efforts are less so. All children should not receive the same education because all children are not created with equal gifts, talents, and abilities. All children are of equal essential value and ought to be treated equally by just law, but the education they receive must take into account the principle of individuality.

This principle is found throughout the ancient books of the Bible. We have already mentioned the following passage in the Song of Songs: "Our sister is young; she has no breasts. What will we do for our sister on the day she is spoken for? If she is a wall, we will build a silver parapet on it. If she is a door, we will enclose it with cedar planks" (8:8–9).

Different children require different training and treatment. The first twins in the Bible were sharply different in personality and ability: "When the boys grew up, Esau became an expert hunter, an outdoorsman, but Jacob was a quiet man who stayed at home" (Gen. 25:27).

Another passage encourages us not to minimize any particular person for the individual gifts he has been given: "Now there are different gifts, but the same Spirit. . . . But one and the same Spirit is active in all these, distributing to each one as He wills" (1 Cor. 12:4, 11). Each person has different gifts and should be appreciated for the gifts he has been given.

Jesus' parable of the talents describes three different individuals who received three different sums of talents (Matt. 25:15–30). They were judged, not by how much they had at the end, but whether they did something with the talents they each received. This principle expresses the importance of capitalizing on the talents given each person, and education should prepare a child to maximize the return on his talents.

Practicing the Principle of Individuality

Parents who understand and live out this principle of individuality will not panic if they happen to have a child who does not learn to read until age ten. This child may even grow up and win a Pulitzer prize for authoring some fine novel. Of course, this level-headed parenting is easier said than done. It is especially difficult to accept the slow starter when another child in the same family is a precocious little prodigy who reads at three and works algebra problems at seven. But parents who know the principle of individuality will relax and enjoy the individual characteristics of each child. They understand that, as with all children, this child will be different from the others. As an artist who realizes that every color in his paint box may not be appropriate to paint some particular scene, so a parent must realize that every academic tidbit of knowledge may not be equally valuable to the shaping of one particular child.

Ultimately, this principle recommends a disconnect of grade level from age. No set of ten-year-old children should be confined to the fifth grade in all subjects. A family with six children will see these children progress at different rates through the sequence of kindergarten through twelfth-grade mathematics. It is not uncommon to find three children from the same family (at ten years of age) studying fourth-grade math, fifth-grade math, and seventh-grade math. Or put another way, it would be highly unusual for a group of six children in the same family to be in the same level of mathematics at the same age if the principle of individuality is properly applied in that family.

This also means that there is no single curriculum program that will work for all children. This is also why a school system should never adopt one particular curriculum and require that curriculum for all children in the system. Despite the fact that you may occasionally meet a salesman or school administrator who endorses a particular academic program or curriculum package as the perfect approach for all people, you need to take such gushing praise for what it is — a sales pitch. One curriculum package will work amazingly well with one particular student, while it will fail miserably with another.

The curriculum or program chosen for any particular child will depend on the parent/mentor's knowledge of that child. There may be a certain amount of trial and error that is exercised in this process. My wife and I have disposed of more than one curriculum package for our children. We have skipped whole grade levels in other packages. We have supplemented some packages with alternate material of our choosing. We watch for boredom. If a child is completing the lesson in fifteen minutes and appears half-asleep while working the lesson, we may skip several hundred pages in the textbook.

We watch for signs of frustration and intimidation. If the lesson is taking an inordinate amount of time to complete or the material is regularly bringing the child to tears, then we either supplement, take a six-month break, or revert back to easier material. This is not a complicated, technical process at all. It only requires a parent or teacher who is tuned in to the child and is willing to be flexible.

Some would take this principle to mean that a child is never to be challenged by difficult material; however, there is nothing wrong with challenging a child. It is frustration and intimidation that should be avoided. A child's ability to accept a challenge is determined to some extent by his character, which again must be preeminent throughout the education process. For example, we regularly subject our younger children to literature (read aloud) that is far above their capacity to understand, usually as we are teaching the older children. This stretches the younger children and can be a good way to extend their potential. But the advanced material is not presented as a standard to which we hold them. They are not shamed if they cannot comprehend the material. Also these challenges are only occasional exercises and do not *characterize* their academic experience.

This approach to education may be intimidating at first. It can shake up a teacher who has grown to appreciate one particular curriculum package or who has adopted one set of lesson plans for a whole career. It may be painful for a parent to take an eleven-year-old child and place him back into a third-grade mathematics program. That parent must utterly believe that this is the beginning of a successful education. The principle of individuality unleashes a powerful recipe for success. In the long run it is the only way that our children will excel in education. Ironically, it is only when children are not forced to travel together that no child will be left behind.

The Principle of Individuality Coming Alive

The recent explosion of free-market activity in the field of education has produced a plethora of educational methods and curriculum approaches. Huge homeschooling conventions around the country allow thousands of parents to review many different curriculum packages. The one-size-fits-all education system is quietly disappearing. What works for one child may not work for another. What works for one family may not work for another. What works for one community may not work for another. The directions recently set by the charter school movement, the homeschool movement, and the private school movement have been *away from standardization.*

This principle of individuality holds profound implications for the involvement of the state in education. It would urge the state to allow much greater latitude for parental choice in education. Politicians who do not include the words *parental choice* in their endless, passionate rhetoric on education are not even approaching real solutions in the field. Inevitably, government control of education leads to centralization and inflexibility, which prevents parents and teachers from optimizing the educational experience for each child. This is why the imposition of sheer centralized power will not solve the education problems of this land. As governments attempt to improve education, they set out to control the one thing that cannot be controlled, thereby squelching any real progress. There is no expert who can set standards for every child, for every family from every cultural background, for every community in this great nation. The temptation for conservatives and liberals alike is to believe that somehow government can improve education by sheer force, using money and control. The truth is, humans do not learn this way. Every child is an individual. Thus every child must receive an individualized program of instruction, whether from a parent or someone else.

This principle presses for *de-centralization* of education, instead of the present prevailing trend to centralize. It cannot be the bureaucrat in

Washington who dictates whether little Johnny is a child with a special need. Only the teacher of that child can tell you Johnny's special need. There is no way that the commissioner of education can determine how one ten-year-old child in Topeka, Kansas, should perform on a nationally standardized test. It is the teacher of that boy who has worked with him for the last four years who should make that call. No U.S. Department of Education official should dictate the standards for a Native-American-populated school in South Dakota in language, math, history, and geography. It is the teachers who labor every day with those children who live in a particular cultural and geographical context who should establish those expectations. The standards should not be a function of national averages, but rather a function of natural ability and progress rates determined on an individual level and defined in broad terms on the basis of individual communities.

This means that the control of education must be transferred *back* into the communities, to the teachers, and to individual families. This transfer must include responsibility, accountability, and testing. The office that distributes the money will inevitably attempt to control the process. After all, that is the other golden rule! He who has the gold makes the rules. The funding of education must ultimately lie in the laps of parents who must control the educational choices they make for their children. Tax credits form better public policy than vouchers for the purposes of true educational choice.

Conclusion

To ignore the all-important principle of individuality in the education of children is like boxing with a cactus plant bare-handed—you will lose! As a nation, we have lost. We will continue to lose in the education of millions of children across this country so long as this principle is ignored by parents, teachers, and lawmakers. It is a powerful principle. Parents who discover this principle and maximize on it *will* find success in the education of each one of their God-sent gifts.

7 The Fifth Time-Tested Secret for a Successful Education:

The Rooting in Relationships

On April 28, 2004, police found a father and his daughter living deep in the forest in the northwest corner of Oregon. Homeless and destitute, the father had opted not to leave his daughter to grow up on the streets. Instead, he took her into the woods, and for four years they lived in a makeshift lean-to against a hillside. Police were amazed to find the girl clean, healthy, and . . . educated! There in the forest, the father had homeschooled his daughter with nothing but a Bible and a decrepit set of encyclopedias. Incredibly, when officials tested the twelve-year-old, they found that she had already achieved a twelfth-grade equivalency. How could this happen without a federal department of education? There were no certified teachers and no expensive curriculum. So what was the secret? Police Sergeant Michael Barkley told reporters, "What was so clear was that their living conditions were unacceptable, but their relationship was a real deep love and caring for each other."[1] There are some factors in the education of a child that transcend all other factors. These factors are so powerful that they eliminate the need for experts, expensive government programs, and extensive regulations. Sadly, they are factors largely ignored by our education systems in place today.

The Fifth Time-Tested Secret for a Successful Education: The Rooting in Relationships

In 1986 I was sitting in the office of a fully tenured professor at a major United States public university, discussing an engineering project assigned in the senior year of the program. I asked this professor if we could meet on a regular basis concerning this project. I sat, stunned, as he answered, "No, no. If I had my druthers, I'd just as soon sit here and contemplate my navel." Years later I realized why almost everyone who took this man's classes produced Ds and Fs. This teacher manifested zero interest in the content of his instruction and even less interest in the students he taught.

There is a difference between human beings and computers. For example, children will occasionally break down and cry while learning math facts. Computers never do this. You cannot stuff information into a child's brain as if he were sixty gigabytes of hard-disk drive space. Human beings are organic creatures, created with a capacity for relationships with God and their fellow men. Any education system that does not take into account this basic feature of the human creature is bound to be a dismal failure.

The last chapter emphasized the vital importance of the principle of individuality in education. That is, every child is an individual with individual abilities, absorption rates, learning patterns, and emotional concerns. An educational program will only be optimized for an individual child by a mentor who knows the child well. In general, who would *know* a child better than his own parents? In most cases, who would *love* a child more than his own parents? Parents invest themselves in their children. In most cases, no one invests more time, resources, emotions, and love in children than their own parents.

At first blush it may appear strange that there is no statistically significant difference between the academic performance of a homeschooled child whose parents are professionally trained, certified teachers and those children whose parents are not state-certified teachers. Yet, this is what repeated studies have shown. There must be something else at work here. It is a powerful principle that has the potential to eclipse the contributions of professional training. It is the God-designed factor of relationship-based teaching.

The importance of parental involvement in the education of a child is generally granted by serious educators. Children whose parents fail to show up at the parent-teacher conferences are almost inevitably the ones who will fail. At some level, a fruitful education requires the involvement of a parent or mentor who has a meaningful relationship with the child.

The Time-Tested Perspective

If you are going to prepare someone for life and eternity, you must establish a relationship. The Bible recommends deep personal involvement when it comes to teaching or discipleship work. Jesus is an important example of a teacher. During the three years of ministry recorded in the Gospels, he spent the time traveling with his students, teaching and ministering to them. He fixed food for them. He told them he loved them. Then he died for them. His ministry of teaching was thoroughly soaked in relationships. The apostle Paul's method was similar: "And that I did not shrink back from proclaiming to you anything that was profitable, or from teaching it to you in public and from house to house. . . . Therefore be on the alert, remembering that night and day for three years I did not stop warning each one of you with tears" (Acts 20:20, 31). For Jesus and Paul, a deep personal involvement was necessary for any meaningful, relationship-based discipleship.

According to the Bible, this principle of relationship-based teaching is especially true in the area of training and educating a child. The biblical principle relating to the training of children is beautifully defined in the *locus classicus* on education:

*These words that I am giving you today are to be in your heart. Repeat them
to your children. Talk about them when you sit in your house and when you
walk along the road, when you lie down and when you get up. Bind them as
a sign on your hand and let them be a symbol on your forehead. Write them
on the doorposts of your house and on your gates. Deuteronomy 6:6–9*

In this ancient Book of the Hebrews and Christians, there are few texts
that address the education of children as directly as this one. There are several
rich principles in this passage. First, the responsibility of education lies solidly
in the laps of parents. This directive is not leveled at the community or "the
village." The Hebrew word used for the phrase "you shall teach them" is given
in the masculine singular. In other words, the text is directed to the father.
Ephesians 6:4 confirms this interpretation, addressing comments relating to
the child's training and education to the father of the children: "Fathers . . .
bring your children up in the nurture and admonition of the Lord" (KJV).
References to the community or the state's involvement in the education of the
child are conspicuously absent from any biblical texts on educating children.
Conversely, the passages that *do* refer to education of children always assume
the parents as responsible (see Deut. 4:9–12; Prov. 1:8; 6:20–21). Other texts
even underscore the importance of a direct involvement of parents in the
education of children: "When your son asks you in the future, 'What is the
meaning of the decrees, statutes, and ordinances, which the LORD our God
has commanded you?' tell him, 'We were slaves of Pharaoh in Egypt, but the
LORD brought us out of Egypt with a strong hand'" (Deut. 6:20–21).

As already mentioned in chapter 3, the entire book of Proverbs is
presented as a father teaching and mentoring a son. Although the father is
the primary responsible agent in the *paideia* of the child in ancient Hebrew
and Christian education, the mother is not neglected. The last chapter of
Proverbs contains the instruction of a mother given to her son.

A Sample of the Addresses Found in the Book of Proverbs

Father Addresses Son (All verses are taken from KJV.)

1:8 — My son, hear the instruction of thy father, and forsake not the law of thy mother:...

1:10 — My son, if sinners entice thee, consent thou not.

1:15 — My son, walk not thou in the way with them; refrain thy foot from their path:...

2:1 — My son, if thou wilt receive my words, and hide my commandments with thee; . . .

3:1 — My son, forget not my law; but let thine heart keep my commandments:...

3:21–22 — My son, let not them depart from thine eyes: keep sound wisdom and discretion: So shall they be life unto thy soul, and grace to thy neck.

4:10 — Hear, O my son, and receive my sayings; and the years of thy life shall be many.

4:20 — My son, attend to my words; incline thine ear unto my sayings.

5:1 — My son, attend unto my wisdom, and bow thine ear to my understanding:...

6:1–2 — My son, if thou be surety for thy friend, if thou hast stricken thy hand with a stranger, thou art snared with the words of thy mouth, thou art taken with the words of thy mouth.

7:1–3 — My son, keep my words, and lay up my commandments with thee. Keep my commandments, and live; and my law as the apple of thine eye. Bind them upon thy fingers, write them upon the table of thine heart.

19:27 — Cease, my son, to hear the instruction that causeth to err from the words of knowledge.

23:15—My son, if thine heart be wise, my heart shall rejoice, even mine.

24:21—My son, fear thou the LORD and the king: and meddle not with them that are given to change:...

Mother Addresses Son

31:2—What, my son? and what, the son of my womb? and what, the son of my vows?

A cursory examination of the ancient record of Solomon's wisdom would conclude that the book is nothing less than *sheer involvement* of a father in the life of his son. Indeed, the book is permeated with personal addresses of a father to a son, often employing emotional and deeply relational language. Throughout, the father instructs his son; but he also pleads, warns, observes, charges, implores, rebukes, and exhorts. The teaching is rooted in an organic relationship. It is intimate, caring, and fatherly. This is an age-old, real-life, divinely inspired example of what is intended for the discipleship and training of a child. The teaching is personal and parental.

The Deuteronomy 6 passage has more instructions relevant to educating our children. The teaching must also be diligent. The key word used in Deuteronomy 6:7 is *repeat*. The Hebrew word used is derived from the word used for sharpening a knife. As one sharpens a blade on a stone, parents are encouraged to teach their children on the words of Jehovah by consistent repetition. The education of a child must also include an integration of that Word into every element of the child's life. Notice that this education is both prepared (v. 6) and spontaneous (vv. 7–8). It occurs at all times of the day and is to be incorporated even into the mundane activities of life. Parents exercise this training in all the varied situations in which any ordinary family might find themselves. In summary, this central text on education holds parents responsible to God to give their children the *"paideia* of the Lord," an education that will prepare them for life in this world and for eternity in heaven.

Evidently, the Lord has a purpose in mind for this involvement of parents in the training of their children. It is the transfer of the faith of the parents to the next generation. This purpose is obvious from a number of different texts in the Bible. In each text, the key purpose stated is italicized (emphasis mine).

> *"God also said to Abraham, 'As for you,* you and your offspring after you *throughout their generations* are to keep My covenant.'"
>
> *Genesis 17:9*

> *"Didn't the one God make us with a remnant of His life-breath? And what does the One seek?* A godly offspring." *Malachi 2:15*

> *"We must not hide them from their children, but must tell a future generation the praises of the LORD, His might, and the wonderful works He has performed. He established a testimony in Jacob and set up a law in Israel, which He commanded our fathers to teach to their children so that a future generation — children yet to be born — might know. They were to rise and tell their children so* that they might put their confidence in God and not forget God's works, but keep His commandments." *Psalm 78:4–7*

This last passage again reiterates the importance of parental teaching. The end, or intended, purpose of this teaching is that children may set their hope in God, remember his works, and keep his commandments. In other words, the objective is a continuing faithfulness to God throughout future generations. The method is by way of fathers communicating to their children. The most powerful form of evangelism available to man happens when a father takes his little boy by the hand and says, "Let me show you Jesus." The ministries of all of the evangelists in the world will never compare to the deep impacting ministries of mothers and fathers who are willing to take on their God-ordained responsibilities to faithfully mentor their children.

Consider how much more can be done when one generation builds upon another! When one father trains his son and encourages him to make wise use of the spiritual talents and heritage he has received, and when this pattern continues for four, five, and six generations, tremendous things can occur in personal character-building, family-building, church-building, and culture-building efforts. It may appear to be a slow and painful process. It may not be spectacular; but in the long run, more will be accomplished this way.

The Nature of the Teacher/Student Relationship

We have already established that the ancient book of Proverbs is dedicated to the topic of educating a young person. It is packed with character lessons communicated to a son by his father and mother. There is far more in this book, however, than character lessons. It contains a penetrating and powerful methodology for education. It is education rooted in a relationship, carried from the heart of a father to the heart of a son. The father's teaching is caring, intimate, open, and honest — even desperate and demanding at points.

But the core of this relational method of education emerges in Proverbs 23:26, where the father bursts out with something of a plea, a demand, and heart-deep desire: *"My son, give me your heart and let your eyes observe my ways"* (italics mine).

It is plain from the context that this is the boy's father speaking, and he is not merely asking for his son's attention. He is after his heart. He wants his son to come close enough to listen to his heart. He wants his son to be close enough to observe his ways. This, of course, assumes that the father has a heart for God and a vision for his kingdom. He tells his son, "Follow me as I lead you to God. Go with me, son! Follow me as I teach you the truth."

Losing the Hearts of Our Children

To some of us this sounds a little like a fantasy world, since we have drifted far from the moorings provided by the age-old principles. But that only makes the issue more relevant. Our hearts cry out again for the hearts of our children, for we sense that these relationships have drifted apart. There are two ways in which the hearts of parents and children are separated.

1. The hearts of the fathers (or mothers) may be cut away from the hearts of the sons (or daughters) when parents do not have the time to invest in their children. Or they may have time to spend, but the time is hurried. Their minds may be disconnected by impacted schedules as they run in all directions after the assorted screaming exigencies of modern life. This may also occur when we have delegated the discipleship and education of our children to others. Or it may occur when we, as parents, have succumbed to habitual sins such as anger, impatience, and selfishness.

2. Relationships between generations are also severed when peer groups and cultural influences of the day form an almost irresistible force to pry away the heart of the child from his parents. Young men and women are easily drawn to the "flakiness" or, as Proverbs puts it, the "foolishness" of the immature rather than to the wisdom of their parents.

A Father and Son

Today, I sat in the car driving home from the office. My twelve-year-old son sat next to me, and I thought back on the years in which our relationship developed into what it is today.

When the doctors pulled that little guy out of the womb (by C-section) almost thirteen years ago, he screamed like a banshee, and just kept on screaming—for years, only taking a breath now and then for eating and sleeping. That's how we were abruptly and a little rudely introduced to parenting so many years ago.

At the beginning, fathering for me involved bringing home a paycheck and planting a good-night kiss on his forehead. I was too busy changing the world, writing books, running for governor of the state, and that sort of thing. I was too busy changing the world to realize that all my activity out in the world couldn't hold a candle to the kind of deep-seated, long-term effect I could have in the life of one solitary little boy. I just kept the door to my office closed so I could concentrate better on changing the world. He was three years old and still screaming a lot.

In those early years, I heard somewhere that it is a good idea to read the Bible as a family, so we began a daily habit of what we called "Bible Time." This was a huge leap in my conception of parenting, although I was later to discover that this fifteen-minute-a-day routine was not enough for me to build a relationship.

My son had a strong will, strong emotions, and a strong mind. He was a difficult boy. When we would ask for counsel from other experienced parents, they would take one look at him and freeze in terror. Days, months, and years of intense training seemed to drag without signs of improvement. Then one day something changed. He had changed. Although still running on high octane during waking hours, there was an edge that was missing. Months after we noticed the change, the little boy came to his mother and said, "Mom, I think that God has given me a white heart." Two parents thanked the Lord with tears in their eyes.

Meanwhile, the corporate ladder in the manufacturing world did not allow much room for my son. The rungs were pretty narrow, and the hours were long. A little five-year-old would tag along on Saturdays to the big corporation. But the security guard would spend more time with him than Daddy would, because Daddy was busy writing reports and supervising the weekend shifts.

After seven years in the corporate world, I began to seek a more efficient way to change the world with what gifts I perceived I had. If it wasn't politics and the corporate world, maybe it was ministry. Leaving the corporate world did allow more time with my family, but ministry is important work. Soon the ministry began to take me away for extended periods of time. Once more my heart was drifting from my home and my son.

When he turned eleven years old, the Lord brought a crisis into our lives that pointed me back to the relationship. After much prayer, we reached the decision that my wife would no longer homeschool our son. He would be with me. He had been surrounded by four little women and a mother every day, and it was obvious that it was going to be pretty tough for him to grow into a man that way. So we decided that we would end his homeschooling right there. From then on, he would car-school, office-school, conference-room -school, and restaurant-school. He would be with me.

Now he lives his life with me. He is close enough every day to see me work and talk and negotiate and pray and disciple. The relationship has grown remarkably close. I love him more than I ever have before. And I think I'm beginning to know a little bit of what it is to disciple a little boy and teach him how to be a man.

Capturing the Hearts of Our Children

The most profound progress in education is achieved when parents or mentors have gained the hearts of their children. There have been moments in my life when I sensed that I was losing the heart of one of my children. Times like these call for action framed in wisdom. Here are a few thoughts that I have found helpful to capturing or recapturing the hearts of our children.

1. *Start early.* There is a critical time frame where we must grapple for the hearts of our children. Generally, this is before the teen

years, when the little ones still want to grow up to be like daddy or mommy.

2. *Reassess priorities.* The modern age presents to us painful choices between such values as relationships and materials, between complexity and simplicity. There is some intuitive truth in that twentieth-century adage: "When you're lying on your death bed, chances are you will not be wishing you had spent more time at the office." May God help us to turn our hearts toward home.

3. *Integrate.* There are ways to integrate our children back into our lives, even if it is as simple as driving together to the grocery store, attending meetings together, cleaning the house, or fixing the car. It only requires the desire, the will, and a little creativity to reintegrate our children back into our lives.

4. *Pave the roads.* Work to establish meaningful conversation with your child. Communicate with him on the things that matter most. Speak to his heart from your heart about your faith and what the Lord has been teaching you from his Word. Establish a regular time in the Word together.

5. *Repave the roads.* You may need to repave the roads of communication. One of the most powerful ways to do this is by simple, heart-felt confession. If you are convicted that you have not been doing something correctly, be honest and open in laying that before your children. Ask for their forgiveness.

6. *Pray and trust in God's grace.* We are always challenged as parents. We are humbled. Even on our best days, we come up short. My two-year-old offers me her little drawing of scribbles. "Wook, Daddy, wook!" she says. My reaction is not to throw it back at her in a rage saying, "What is this? Just a bunch of scribbles on a piece of paper? Take it away!" No. I take her up in my arms and say,

"Thank you, sweetheart! You drew this for me?" I post it over my desk. She gave me a little piece of her heart. She wanted to please me with the drawing, and she is pleased when she sees that I am pleased. Similarly, when we parents, as the adopted children of our heavenly Father, present our hearts to the Lord in prayer and in humble obedience to his Word, he accepts us. When we present our parenting work to God as scribbles on a piece of paper, we must believe that he will accept it and that his grace will cover us. We must believe that when God posts our grubby, blotchy artwork, he really can turn it into something great. It is only then that we realize what we really mean when we cry out to our children, "My son, give me your heart!"

Mind, Emotions, and Will

There is one more significant text that speaks to the method by which *paideia,* or education, within the close father-son relationship must occur: "As you know, like a father with his own children, we encouraged, comforted, and implored each one of you" (1 Thess. 2:11).

Three words used here meet each of the aspects of a human being: *exhortation* calls the will to practical obedience; *comforting* is an appeal to the emotions of the child; and *charging* (or better translated, "testifying") is an appeal to the mind. A relationship is required when making an appeal to the will or to the emotions. An unemotional lecture can dump intellectual material on the brain. The problem is that a human being is far more than a mind. Each person has emotions and a will. If he is going to respond in any practical way to what he hears in mind, emotions, and will, then the whole person must be addressed. Children learn well when they are nurtured, when you hold them on your lap and kiss them. They cannot be treated as mechanical robots and processed through a bureaucratized educational program.

The Heart of the Mentor

Learning is couched in relationships. The quality of the relationship will determine the quality of the education. What is needed is a deep-seated, long-term relationship. The more profound the lesson taught and the more significant and permanent the effects of an educational experience, the deeper the teacher-student relationship must become. Discipline or correction, for example, is not taken well from an administrator who has not spent the time paving the connecting path between hearts. As in all relationships, love is the key. Love begins with a sincere desire to bring about the best for the child, such that the child knows the mentor seeks that end. The mentor has a vested interest in the child's success, and the child knows it. Love usually involves some kind of sacrifice in terms of emotions, time, or effort. It is a long-term investment. Love is expressed in both word and action. It comes through discipline, tears, encouragement, understanding, and prayer for the minds and souls of our children. It comes by example, by an open ear, by trials and conflicts, and in the resolution of conflicts.

A good teacher assumes responsibility for his students regardless of their abilities, attitudes, and backgrounds. In my experiences, there will be insufficient vested interest in each student without a loving relationship with that student that has been tried and tested true.

The Role of Delegation

Can a parent delegate the work of education to someone else? This is the major question families must address as they choose between conventional schooling and home-based education. The question is more difficult when one considers that it is not an all-or-nothing question. Some level of delegation may be appropriate without *completely* delegating the task. From the beginning, delegation has occurred in the education of young people. Jesus, at twelve years of age, sat in the temple with the doctors of the law for at least a day, listening to them and asking them questions (see Luke 2:42).

The responsibility for the *paideia* (training and education) of children rests on the shoulders of parents. Perhaps this responsibility can be understood using the following illustration. Let us say that God was the president of the "Raising Children Operation," overseeing families all over the world. If he were to see a problem with the education of one particular child, he would not call the child's Sunday school teacher or his day school teacher into the front office for a discussion on the matter. According to Ephesians 6:4, it is the *father* who is held responsible. This does not eliminate delegation, but even when some of the work of educating our children is delegated to others, the responsibility for the work performed still lies with the parent(s). Therefore, parental oversight of the delegated work is crucial.

The following is a brief summary of the factors parents should take into consideration as they delegate.

1. *The education of children in the Bible occurs predominantly in the family.* Every passage dealing with the training of children directs itself to parents. Deuteronomy 6 specifically details situations in which the training needs to take place, and those situations are obviously home-based situations (sitting in home, lying down, rising up). Most teaching situations patterned in the Bible are discussions between fathers and sons. Although the children are included in the large assembly of the congregation while the Word of God is taught and read, according to the following passage from Deuteronomy 4, God's Law/Word is taught to the people in order that they might do two things with it—*obey the Word and go home and teach their children that Word:*

   Only be on your guard and diligently watch yourselves, so that you don't forget the things your eyes have seen and so that they don't slip from your mind as long as you live. Teach them to your children and your grandchildren. The day you stood before the LORD your God at Horeb, the LORD said to me, "Assemble the people before Me, and I will let them hear My words, so that they may learn to fear Me all the days they live on the earth and may instruct their children." (vv. 9–10, emphasis mine)

2. *Children are simultaneously impressionable and deeply indebted to their parents during their early years.* If I were to tell my four-year-old daughter that the moon was made out of cheese and accessible to her by a very large spoon, she would be outside the next evening with the longest spoon she could find. Those children raised in a proper Christian home experience no greater human love than that which they see poured out by their parents. There is hardly a person on Earth whom a child would be more likely to follow than the one who loves her the most.

3. *The nature of the lessons to be taught will determine the degree of delegation.* For example, a complete stranger might be able to teach a child some isolated fact, such as the capital city of China. The depth, significance, and personal relevance of a message are the factors that heighten the importance of relationship in education. Any lesson that will be important to a child's spiritual, emotional, and intellectual development should be taught in a close-knit relationship. That is why the Bible establishes the *paideia* of a child in the parent-child relationship as normative. This is also why, for example, corporal punishment from a loving parent is more effective than the same punishment from a disconnected relative or friend of the family, or why an appeal to the conscience of the child would be more effective from a parent than it would be from a stranger.

4. *There is serious risk in delegating part of your child's education to other teachers.* Whether parents are considering delegating a single course or an entire program (by using an institutional school), they are still responsible to carefully familiarize themselves with the curriculum, the teachers, and the peer contact involved before making the final decision to delegate. If the teaching is known to be in error or the teacher is known to have ideological or practical weaknesses, then the parent is absorbing even more risk and may not be able to sufficiently correct the error that the child encounters.

5. *With age, a child grows in his ability to discern between truth and error.* Most young children are unable to identify and counter subtle philosophical messages representing serious error, relating to origins, psychology, environmentalism, gender roles, and many other areas. There are serious and fundamental conflicts today in the realm of ideas, and these really do cross over into education and will impact our children's future in life and eternity. (We will develop this point in chapter 11.) The risk involved in delegation should decrease as the child matures. Ideally, a parent should be able to trust a child to stand up to negative peer influences and ideas that subvert his worldview sometime between twelve and eighteen years of age.

6. *The principle of individuality must be considered when delegating as well.* More care must be taken with the "doors," than with the "walls" (Song of Songs 8:9).

Implications of This Powerful Principle

The question that all parents need to ask themselves as they make that all-important decision regarding how they will educate their children is this: "How can we maximize the relationship principle in the education of this child?" In other words, is there a fruitful relationship already established in the child's life upon which we can build an effective education?

Obviously, homeschooling is a natural application of the principle. Although there are some people who perhaps cannot homeschool (maybe 1 percent to 10 percent of the population), many who think they cannot do it have never really seriously considered it, or they have never tried it. Every day, increasing numbers of parents are discovering that they *can* do it and *do it well*. Between 1.7 and 2 million children are currently homeschooled in this country. If there is even a possibility that it might work, I recommend that a family try it for at least one year. Even if home education is not a viable possibility with a family, this does not mean that the principle of relationships in education is lost. A child may still receive a successful education if serious efforts are made to maximize on this principle of relationship-based learning.

What does this principle mean for schools? The teacher-child relationship will always be the keystone to success for any school. At some point, large classrooms work against this principle. Moreover, the modern approach to education in which children move from classroom to classroom, with a different teacher every hour, and where they receive different teachers every year is a blatant violation of this principle. A teacher should take into account her relationship with each student. She can measure her own effectiveness in the classroom by the quality of relationship she has established with each individual student. School administrators and teachers should never negate the importance of parental involvement. Teachers should always strongly encourage significant parental involvement. I recommend regular communication with parents and opening classrooms up to parental presence and assistance. All means should be employed to encourage parental involvement in academic decision-making, especially in the tailoring of the education to each individual child.

The reader may have noted by now that the recommendations of this book generally oppose the trends seen in education over the last century. Layers of bureaucracy have increasingly removed parental involvement and control in education. Teachers are more strapped than ever by regulations and state control. All of this leads to a gradual disintegration of real education and the proper development of children in each successive generation.

What Happened to Relationships?

Over the last two hundred years, several influential philosophers have contributed to the social situation in which we find ourselves today, but none holds as influential a position as the French political philosopher Jean Jacques Rousseau. He is the father of modern political theory, socialist revolutions, and modern statist education. Upon the birth of his first child in 1746, he promptly persuaded his young wife, Therese, to abandon the child on the steps of an orphanage. Sadly, he kept up this *modus operandi* with every one of his five children. Seven years after abandoning his fifth child, he wrote a book titled *Emile,* a landmark book introducing a modern form of education. Historians Will and Ariel Durant summarize this monumental work in these words: "Roussaeau wanted a system of public instruction by the state. He prescribed many years with an unmarried tutor, who would withdraw the child as much as possible from parents and relatives."[2] Another modern historian, Paul Johnson, comments on Rousseau's creation: "Rousseau asserts that brooding on his conduct towards his children led him eventually to formulate the theory of education he put forward in *Emile.* . . . What began as a process of personal self-justification gradually evolved, as repetition and growing self-esteem hardened them into genuine convictions, into the proposition that education was the key to social and moral improvement and this being so, it was the concern of the State. By a curious link of infamous moral logic,

Rousseau's iniquity as a parent was linked to his ideological offspring, the future totalitarian State."[3]

The current system does not appear in a vacuum. All social consequences rest upon the ideas and philosophers of the past. Is it possible that the quiet abandonment of that keystone of relationships in a child's education can be traced back to the mind of a man who abandoned his own children and justified it in his political philosophy? After severing the relationships of father and children in his own home, he proceeded to sever that relationship in his social theories. It is a breathtaking revelation that such a man as this should have such tremendous influence on modern educational theory. In the words of one conventional history of the philosophy of education, "Highly debatable though [Rousseau's] propositions are, they have had immense influence on educational theory, including the 'progressive education' formulated by John Dewey (1889–1952) and his followers."[4] Debatable propositions indeed, but highly influential. Rousseau's orphans are everywhere today.

There is another explanation for the decline in deep, fruitful relationships and the mechanization of education over the last two centuries. The industrial revolution brought great material blessings to the modern world, but not without a cost. In 1850 human existence very much consisted of close relationships within family and community. Charity was privatized, neighbors talked, and families grew up together. Typical of most young boys in the 1870s, Almanzo Wilder, in *Farmer Boy* by Laura Ingalls Wilder, plowed the fields next to his father. Most of life's lessons were learned in those fields. As the industrial revolution came on like a hurricane, the fathers of Almanzo's world sold their farms and moved to the big city for corporate jobs. The division of labor afforded by the industrial revolution enabled the teaching profession to burgeon. The public school systems further enabled this trend. Eventually mother left home for her corporate position to sustain the standard of living strained by the rising cost of inflation and taxation. Taxes were raised from

10 percent of the people's income (in 1910) to about 50 percent (by the 1980s) to pay for expensive social programs such as education for children and social security for retired parents. Meanwhile, family relationships continued to fragment. Gradually public schools turned away from the one-room schoolhouse into segregated classes, further segregating the family throughout the day. Extra-curricular programs and churches added more age-segregated programs throughout the week. Noninteractive and impersonal forms of entertainment were developed, beginning with television and then video and computer games, further undermining opportunities for conversation and relationship building.

A cumulative result of these changes introduced by the industrial revolution was the disintegration of the family. Now, 150 years later, advertisements for cell phones feature families trying to arrange meetings for an occasional ten-minute rendezvous at a fast-food restaurant. My purpose here is not to condemn any particular product of the industrial revolution. Neither is the solution to be found in a return to an agrarian society. That would be impractical and unnecessary. The point is that all of these developments of the industrial revolution have worked together to bring about serious fragmentation of the family. In aggregate, they have stripped away the opportunity for quality relationship building within the most basic social unit of all — the family.

There is a tendency for certain social trends that develop in history to displace the unchanging principles of life given by God. Back in the days of Jesus, the Pharisees had concocted a system known as "Corban." On the surface it was not a bad idea. A devout Jew could dedicate his life and all his goods to the temple in an act of sacrificial piety. The problem was that this system resulted in a son neglecting his father and mother in their old age. Jesus attacked this system, charging that they had squeezed out the principle of God's Word by these human traditions (Matt. 25:1–10). This is always a risk we run with traditions. Not all traditions are bad. Sometimes certain traditions that appear in family life, church life, and in any human institution may begin to distract us from the vital principle. We must, therefore, be sensitive to this human tendency. In every age, men and women ought to question inherited traditions, determining how those traditions either encourage or discourage the implementation of the ancient and unchanging principles.

There is no question in my mind that the homeschooling movement is a radical reaction to the trends of the industrial revolution of the last 150 years. It is an attempt to reintegrate families, the most basic social unit. Are there additional ways to reintegrate the family? Are there ways in which we can creatively repave relationships within the family for a better upbringing for our children? Yes! The same industrial revolution that pulled folks away from the home is now putting them back into the home. Recent studies indicate that telecommuting has risen 25 percent over the last ten years. Churches are working to reintegrate families through the burgeoning "Uniting Church and Family" movement. Some of the largest nonprofits in the Western world, such as Focus on the Family, broadcast programs and publish resources to revive these relationships. Their intent is to reestablish strong marriages and strong families at a time when single-parent birth rates and divorce rates are the highest in the nation's history.

The industrial revolution also brought about great geographical distances between families. In many cases grandparents live far away from their grandchildren. In our family we began to see this as a serious loss. Our children did not enjoy the blessing of time with grandparents throughout the year. So we came up with a solution. It happens that Grandma teaches piano professionally, and our children needed piano lessons. We bought a high-quality telephone headset and for the last three years each child has had a weekly, forty-five-minute lesson with their grandmother over the phone. This has done wonders in the lives of our children. Grandpa usually jumps on the line as well, and they have a good time together.

We are a long way from where we used to be. In many ways, technology has fooled us into thinking that everything now is new and improved. We thought the industrial revolution would make everything more efficient. In the end, there were some things that could not be made more efficient: the relationship developed and the lessons learned by a son as he plowed the fields side by side with his father under the hot summer sun; the time spent on the front porch between grandmother and granddaughter as they snapped the beans and peeled the apples; or the long winter nights shared by a family in close quarters, playing the fiddle, reading out loud by candlelight, and maybe even telling a tall tale or two. With all our technology, division of labor, and efficiency, we have come to discover that we cannot manufacture relationships as we do everything else. There are some things you simply cannot delegate. There are some things you cannot make more efficient by mass production. There are some things you cannot automate. It will always be that way. That is the way it was designed. That is the way the Owner's manual describes its operation.

There are some things we cannot live without, family relationships being one of them. Most certainly, we cannot return to the past. We can find new ways to bring the old ways back in an age of technology. We can learn to integrate our children back into our lives. But this will only happen as we find value in those old principles that placed relationships above all else in this world. Only then will we discover what it is to disciple the heart of a child. Only then will education blossom into something beautiful and redeeming in the life of a child.

How I'm Learning to Be a Father

Over the years that I have raised my son, I have stumbled upon a few things about parent-child relationships.

The first thing I have learned about relationships is that this is really how you change the world. Jesus turned the world upside down by spending three years discipling twelve. Those of us blessed with families find that it is our families that equip us for success in the world. It is the success I enjoy in my familial relationships that provides a basis for success elsewhere. In the words of Paul, "If anyone does not know how to manage his own household, how will he take care of God's church?" (1 Tim. 3:5).

The second thing I have learned is that relationships take time. There is really no such thing as a quality ten minutes here and there. My son and I are together for hours and hours now every day. We travel together quite often. Actually, we really don't talk that much. We sit quietly, comfortably, occasionally commenting on a news story, something he just read, a phone call, a billboard, a challenging business decision, the price of eggs, or what a great wife I've married. Discipling a child really does involve teaching the Word diligently every day as we walk by the way, as we rise up, as we lie down, as we sit in our house, and as we drive in the car (Deut. 6:7).

The third thing I have learned is that I am not an E.D. (Executive Director) of a nonprofit organization. I'm a D.A.D. who happens to be an E.D. My dadness is more defining of who I am. When people used to ask me what I do, I would tell them I was an engineering manager. It took years before I found out that I was first a husband and a father and, oh yes, a few other things.

The fourth thing I have learned from my relationship with my son is that there is a connection between God and Dad in my son's mind. My son may do something for me, and he may do it for God. My son wants to make me proud. I can see him trying hard to please me. Of course, I do not want him to do things for love and honor of Dad and not do them for love and honor of God; but it is plain to me that if he learns to do things for the love of his father, that will do a great deal to propel him towards a relationship with his heavenly Father. The Fifth Commandment is thus connected to the First. If a son does not learn to love and honor his father, how will he learn to love and honor his heavenly Father?

The fifth thing I have learned about relationships is that God does things in me so he can do things in my son. Relationships run in two ways. When setting out to train a son, you begin with a very imperfect little boy. But that's not the only problem. You also have a very imperfect daddy in the equation. In this discipling relationship, I have on many an occasion come face to face with a challenging question: "Do you really love this boy? How much do you love him?"

But this isn't the only question I have had to face. I have heard a question asked in earnest, and it sounded like the voice of Jesus in John 21:15: "Do you really love me?"

I replied, "You know that I love you, my Savior."

Nudging me back to my son, Jesus tells me through his Word, "Then feed my lamb. Love my lamb."

That was when I discovered that my love for Jesus has a lot to do with my love and discipleship of my son. The power of relationships and discipleship has more to do with love than anything else.

The sixth thing I have learned about the father-son relationship is that my son is basically going to turn out like me. I hear him praying, and he sounds like me. I hear him speak in an impatient tone to his sisters; and even as I correct him, I think to myself, *I think I recognize that tone.* Seized by horror for a brief moment, I realize that he is turning out like *me.*

That brings up the seventh thing I have learned from our relationship. I am showing my son how to live, how to struggle, and how to engage the warfare. When he was young, I used outside constraints to engage the warfare for him. I fought his battles for him by discipline, rules, and structure. I could demonstrate my internal struggles over his soul through prayer and exhortation, but I was still fighting for him.

When he grew older, I found that I needed to show him how to engage the struggle. With increasing levels of transparency, I show him more of my own struggles against the world, the flesh, and the devil. I must demonstrate the life of confession and repentance for him because he's going to grow to be an imperfect man just like his daddy.

As we stand side by side in the struggles of life, I tell him, "Watch me, son." I swing the sword a few times. I get down on my knees and cry out to God for help. Then I turn to my son and say, "Now, son, it's your turn to pray. You take the sword and swing it yourself because it's your fight now."

I ask him from time to time, "Are you fighting it, son, or do you want me to fight this one for you?"

He tells me, "I sure am fighting it, Dad. I read God's Word this morning, and I think I'm stronger than I was yesterday."

So here we are, two warriors riding home together again. One of us may still be a tad shorter than the other; but our hearts are knit together in the same battle, the same faith, and the same vision by the same Lord.

8 The Sixth Time-Tested Secret for a Successful Education:
The Principle of Doing the Basics Well

The father and daughter living in the woods of Oregon for four years took the authorities by surprise. They were amazed to find the young daughter clean, in good health, and "well-spoken beyond her years."[1] Their only curriculum was a Bible and an old set of *World Book* encyclopedias. Without a department of education, professionally trained teachers, access to the Internet, standardized curriculum, and the "optimal learning environment," this little twelve-year-old girl had achieved a twelfth-grade academic level. Deep in the Northwest woods, this family found a principle lost in a world where drug education, global warming, social studies, recycling, and computer education make up the essential curriculum.

The Sixth Time-Tested Secret for a Successful Education: The Principle of Doing the Basics Well

Character is the most basic constituent of an educational program. Without character, any other educational effort is an exercise in futility. But education is more than character. It extends into the cultivation of the mind. If the cultivation of the mind is important, then what does one do to cultivate the mind? What is the tried-and-true, basic process of education?

Once again, there are plenty of experts with assorted theories on what constitutes a good education. Education should prepare a child to think, read, write, and speak. There are many different ways to teach a child to do these things. There are also various categories of thinking, reading, writing, and speaking. Children have individual learning styles. Some children will spend more time learning to think on the right side of their brain (with art and music), while others will spend more time learning to think on the left side of their brain (with mathematics and logic). These subject areas are methods by which children learn *how* to think. Some children will be better trained as lawyers to argue a point, other children will be trained to teach a point, while still others will be better trained to negotiate a point. But all must learn to communicate. These are the basics of education.

Reading and Writing

It is significant that God chose the written form of communication as the means to reveal eternal truth to men. After all, he could have communicated to men by word of mouth, audiocassette, or videotape. He could have chosen to communicate by oral tradition from generation to generation. But it is instructive to any theory of education that the vehicle by which he chose to communicate truth to men from ancient times was a book. The books of Moses, written around the fifteenth century BC, are among the earliest writings known to man. Manuscripts of these books from the Qumran caves date back several centuries before Christ.

Without question, writing was God's idea from the beginning of the enscripturation of the Bible. "The LORD then said to Moses, 'Write this down on a scroll as a reminder and recite it to Joshua: I will completely blot out the memory of Amalek under heaven'" (Exod. 17:14; 34:27; Deut. 27:3). If writing was essential, then the reading of that writing was just as essential. The business of writing and reading has been important for every family since Moses wrote the book of Deuteronomy thirty-five hundred years ago: "These words that I am giving you today are to be in your heart. Repeat them to your children. Talk about them when you sit in your house and when you walk along the road, when you lie down and when you get up. Bind them as a sign on your hand and let them be a symbol on your forehead. *Write them on the doorposts of your house and on your gates*" (Deut. 6:6–9, italics mine; see also 11:18–20).

This quintessential passage for parenting outlines the basic principles of education. It commends the *fundamentals* of a good education – reading and writing. This is from a text made crystal clear millennia ago! While the essential content of education is God's words, the practical knowledge that must be provided in that education is writing and reading. It is remarkable to find a theory of education laid out as early as 1500 BC. The assumption made here is that these ancient texts speak authoritatively and relevantly to our situation. These are ancient laws, with far more precedent as educational theory than any other philosophy, whether it be from Plato, Rousseau, Montessori, Dewey, or any other education philosopher of modern times. But more than that, these ancient words speak with authority that only God himself could possess. The education of reading and writing is essential for the people of God. In principle, every father should be able to write so he can write those eternal truths on the posts of his house. Ideally, every child in every household needs to read so he can read those words his father wrote on the posts of his house. This passage also clearly implies that it was God's intention from the beginning that at least portions of his Word be readily accessible to every person. There is a purpose for reading and writing. It is to read and write eternal, revealed truth so as to keep it fresh in the mind of successive generations. God's Word was always meant to be a public matter (see Deut. 27:1–8; 31:19–22).

This is one principle that was revived in the time of the Reformation and Renaissance. It played a major part in the founding of America. As early as 1642, the colony of Massachusetts enacted a law requiring the heads of households to teach children and apprentices to read. The purpose of such legislation was to "insure the religious welfare of their children."[2] Five years later the General Court of Massachusetts provided for the establishment of reading schools because it was "one chief project of that old deluder, Satan, to keep men from the knowledge of the Scriptures."[3] The early American theory of education was simple: *Teach children to read so they can read the Bible.* The age-old principle passed down from Moses was a pivotal part of early American education theory and was a motivating factor in the establishment of the American education institution.

Teach the Basics Well

A good education will teach a child to read well and write well. A recent study, released by the National Institute for Literacy, found that about half of American adults were functionally illiterate, unable to read or comprehend at an eighth-grade level.[4] Our young people may learn a great deal about a good number of subjects, but sadly they are not learning to read well. This puts these students at a severe disadvantage. Most students, with very few exceptions, should be able to read a chapter of this length in about ten minutes. In my experience teaching in public and private schools, it is rare to find high-school students who can read any particular text relatively rapidly and smoothly. It is also rare to find students who like to read.

From the beginning of my family's homeschooling experience, we have emphasized reading as the fundamental part of our curriculum. As a result, by the time my children are ten years old, they are able to read aloud as well as any adult.

When one cannot focus, he cannot do anything well. The Bible prescribes focus and excellence: "Whatever your hands find to do, do with all your strength" (Eccl. 9:10). Therefore, in education, the first critical decision is to identify the thing on which to focus — the fundamentals of character and reading. Then children are taught to focus and to do the fundamentals *well*. The following is a list of ten time-tested, sure-fire methods by which a parent/teacher may ensure a good basic education.

1. Read aloud as much as possible. Parents may read to children or the children may read to each other. The optimum schedule would provide for as much as one to two hours per day of this.

2. Always choose the best literature you can find. Here is a simple test: Any book that is reprinted after two hundred years is usually the best literature. The two books that have been reprinted more than any other books are the Bible and *Pilgrim's Progress.*

3. Do not waste any significant time doing anything but the basics.

4. Do not multiply course requirements upon the student. One highly successful curriculum approach used in many homeschools around the country requires reading a classic book of literature, writing an essay, and completing a mathematics assignment. This simple approach puts these homeschooled students far ahead of their counterparts by the time they are ready for college. A small canoe can make it down the river of education faster than the riverboat with all of its extra amenities.

5. Children should memorize portions of the highest quality literature, poetry, drama, and prose (see Deut. 31:19–22; Ps. 119:11).

6. Children learn to write best when they copy the most excellent literature of all (see Deut. 6:9; 17:18).

7. As children become more advanced in their ability to read their own language, it is advantageous to teach them to read the source languages of Hebrew, Greek, and Latin.

8. Never advance a student to the next level of learning until he has thoroughly mastered the basics. Do not advance a student to the multiplication tables before he has thoroughly learned his addition tables. Never advance a student beyond the first level of reading in the English language before he has thoroughly learned the seventy

phonograms (letters or combination of letters) and forty phonemes (phonetic sounds).

9. Basic learning requires disciplined repetition (see Isa. 28:10–11). The more basic, the more intensive the repetition. This also applies to character lessons. The most basic character lesson is obedience. It is a lesson that is taught thousands of times in the first two years of a child's life, and it continues to a lesser extent for the rest of his life.

10. Teach the ancient Scriptures, the most basic textbook of all (see Deut. 6:6–9; 11:18–21; 27:1–8). If you only have thirty minutes each day to invest in your children's education, spend that time teaching them the Bible.

Thinking

The purpose of education is to prepare a child for life. Therefore, its primary purpose must be to give the child tools to make it through life. This includes strength of character but also the wisdom to make the right decisions. This takes the proper working of the mind. He will need to find solutions to problems in real life, whether those solutions address business/economic problems, relationship-related problems, political problems, or problems related to the physical world. In any decision, he must reject one approach in favor of another. Education will not give him a list of solutions for every possible problem he meets, but it should give him the *tools* to solve those problems.

The student should be trained to draw conclusions from premises and make applications from multiple general principles. Simply stated, as the student progresses through his academic work, he should be able to figure things out on his own.

I was fifteen years old when I hit a wall in high-school algebra. The problem was factoring trinomials. I was working out of a poorly written textbook while homeschooling on the island of Kyushu in the Pacific Ocean. My options for assistance were limited. There was only one person I knew who might be able to help — my father. Unfortunately, his algebra was a little rusty, and he could not help much. So I set out on my own to work out a highly useful method for doing the factoring. I worked it through my mind over and over again. Within a few days it was done. I had the method down, a method I would use in later years when I tutored college and high-school algebra. This represented a significant breakthrough in my learning, but not because I had learned to factor trinomials. I had learned *how to learn.*

Discernment

"For though by this time you ought to be teachers, you need someone to teach you again the basic principles of God's revelation. You need milk, not solid food. Now everyone who lives on milk is inexperienced with the message about righteousness, because he is an infant. But solid food is for the mature — for those whose senses have been trained to distinguish between good and evil." Hebrews 5:12–14

Ideally there should be less dependence on the teacher as a student matures. He should be able to make his own decisions and draw his own applications in the varied situations of life. This maturation is marked by an ability to discern between good and evil, what is true and what is false. According to this important passage in Hebrews, the mature student should be able to draw distinctions, make logical inferences, and make applications from multiple principles, especially in his ethical decisions.

Learning how to reason is one of the basics of learning. Therefore, any academic coursework should include training in the area of critical thinking, logic, methods of research, geometry, and mathematics.

Students should be encouraged to find the answer on their own. They should learn how to take the first several steps of learning or reasoning on their own. The tutorial assistance that is provided should demonstrate the *method* of learning, rather than giving the answers or depositing more facts on the student. If, for example, a question should arise about a black hole during dinner table conversation, the curious child should be sent to the encyclopedia or to the Web immediately for the answer. Children should be trained to comfortably traverse the paths of learning and employ methods of reasoning and research.

Verbal Communication

The third constituent of a basic education is speaking. Just as reading, writing, and thinking must utterly permeate a child's educational experiences, so also must the area of speech. A successful education will include excellence in communication. A child must learn to communicate clearly and persuasively. It is a lifetime effort. The goal is to bring a child to the point that he can function in all of the most likely relationships in which he will find himself in his future. The average child must be prepared for marriage, raising children, serving customers, and church relationships. As the young person matures, he must be prepared to communicate in formal and informal greetings, providing basic exhortations and encouragements, storytelling, telephone conversations, conflict resolution, delegating responsibilities, receiving orders from superiors, and negotiating in trade. If these are not thoroughly covered in a child's education, the program has missed the basics.

First Peter 3:15–16 says: "But set apart the Messiah as Lord in your hearts, and always be ready to give a defense to anyone who asks you for a reason for the hope that is in you. However, do this with gentleness and respect." The art of rhetoric is exercised when a student learns to give that reason to *every* man. The word *every* typically stands for "all kinds" of people. Herein is the challenge. This will only happen when the student has access to others outside his own age group, outside his own family, and outside his own immediate social group. There is a progression through the curriculum of the basics, and this progression is developed further in chapter 12.

Music

Some might question whether artistic expression should be included under the rubric of a basic education, but there is a form of art that is *required* of all of God's people in the Bible—music. The expression that all of God's people were expected to learn as early as the exodus was the art of singing (Exod. 15:21; refer also to 1 Chron. 16:9; 2 Chron. 23:13; Ps. 9:11; 30:4; 47:6; 68:4). Each of our children are learning to play the piano. For some reason God created our voices with varying pitches. Therefore, our family has spent the last several years learning to sing in parts. Even the young children are learning an ear for music and at the same time are learning to sing beautifully before the Lord.

Multiple studies have been conducted on the importance of music in an educational program, and all of them find it to be crucial. But that is not the reason why it should be included in the list of the basic constituents of an optimal educational program. It belongs there because God defines success and what will bring about success in the *paideia* of a child; without question, singing is not an option.

Conclusion

The goal of education is to prepare a child to address the problems of life with his own mind and his own words. Education is not complicated. It only becomes complicated when we forget to focus on the basics. If a child has been taught to read, think, communicate, and sing, he will be able to learn more about the world around him on his own. He will be able to worship God. He will be able to function in life, and he will be successful in the varied experiences and environments into which life will lead him. But this will only happen if he is taught to *do the basics well.*

The Seventh Time-Tested Secret for a Successful Education:
The Principle of Life Integration

If your daughter receives a very good education, by the time she is 24 years old she knows the derivative of a cosine. She knows how Freudian psychology differs from Skinner's.

She knows who Rome fought in the Punic Wars. She knows that Plato asserts ideal forms as an absolute and eternal reality of which the phenomena of the world are a transitory reflection. She knows how pinocytic vesicles function in an amoeba. She knows how to parse just about any Latin verb—and that is only if she's received a *very good education.*

However, more likely than not she will be clueless on how to manage a staff of seven in a home, or how to handle a budget of $100,000 a year without running the household into the ground. She won't know how to cook a meal, how to hire a contractor, how to raise children, how to change diapers, how to calm a baby, how to nurture a two-year-old, how to exercise authority, how to create a budget, how to cut food costs by 40% without wasting fuel, or how to train a five-year-old in social skills. She will not know how to maintain vehicles, how to assess value in products and services, or how to decorate a house. She won't know how to engage in hospitality with skill, wisdom, and grace. She won't know how to do 98% of life. But, did I say that she knows how to parse just about any Latin verb?

Children learn to parse Latin verbs, but for what reason? Of course, it is to read and to comprehend and to communicate by rhetorical means. But why does your daughter need to read and communicate? The answer for Christians should be obvious. She must be able to read the Bible in Greek or Latin or even English, so that she might be able to teach her children to love God and keep His commandments!

Knowledge is one thing, but knowledge without the ability to apply that knowledge is useless and often counter-productive. In the proper education of a child, we must teach two things. We teach them knowledge, and then we teach them *how to apply that knowledge* to life.

The Seventh Time-Tested Secret for a Successful Education: The Principle of Life Integration

What is knowledge anyway? If education operates in the area of knowledge, then it would make sense to define knowledge. Philosophers tell us that *knowledge* is a justified, true belief. But if knowledge is a belief, then we need to define *belief*. As it turns out, the Bible has a great deal to say about faith or belief.

Knowledge or belief from a Christian worldview is more than facts stuffed in a brain. From a biblical perspective, bare knowledge is insufficient. Knowledge or belief must bring some kind of action with it. This is the point of James when he said, "Faith without works is dead" (2:26). True religion cannot be reduced to head knowledge, so genuine faith must include action. For an example of that "faith" action, James suggests visiting the orphans and widows in their affliction. Moreover, action based on knowledge is the capstone to knowledge. "For if anyone is a hearer of the word and not a doer, he is like a man observing his natural face in a mirror; for he observes himself, goes away and immediately forgets what kind of man he was. But he who looks into the perfect law of liberty and continues in it, and is not a forgetful hearer but a doer of the work, this one will be blessed in what he does" (James 1:23–24 NKJV). The one who simply hears the ideas of the Word receives some kind of a superficial knowledge of the truth. If he does not follow up with an active practice of the Word, James concludes that he never really knew it at the first. The superficial learning experience is characterized by the man who glances at himself in the mirror, gets an idea of what he looks like, and then walks away and quickly forgets the image. Truth, according to the Bible, is practical. In fact, Jesus goes so far as to say, "But anyone who *lives by the truth* comes to the light, so that his works may be shown to be accomplished by God" (John 3:21). Truth is not something that sits there and looks at you. Truth is something that is *done*. It is acted out. Several examples should suffice to illustrate the point.

What is love? Is defining the term enough to really know what love is, or is there more to it? The philosopher of the modern age, Jean Jacques Rousseau, was the man who threw away his five children on the steps of an orphanage. Yet he made an astonishing claim: "I was born to be the best friend that ever existed. . . . No one ever had more talent for loving."[1] But, of course, he did not know the first thing about love. One may study every book in the world about love or travel the globe lecturing on love, but he really knows little about love until he has loved the unlovable. You do not know love unless and until you have sacrificed your pride, your comforts, your wealth, or your life for the love of a friend.

Those with the most penetrating understanding of forgiveness are those who have forgiven one who brought irreparable harm upon their children or themselves. Jesus understood it. "Father forgive them because they do not know what they are doing" (Luke 23:34).

We could talk about love and forgiveness all day long for the next forty years, but we can never truly know these principles until they have been integrated into life, until they have been lived. Action based in knowledge is the seal on knowledge, providing permanence, depth, and clarity to that knowledge.

Another way to look at this is by distinguishing between knowledge and wisdom. Wisdom is the application of knowledge to life. Wisdom is vitally important to the young man or young woman. You can almost hear the father in Proverbs crying out with unrelenting insistence: "Wisdom is supreme—so get wisdom. And whatever else you get, get understanding" (4:7). It is the way to walk in life and the road to success. The voice of wisdom speaks: "I walk in the way of righteousness, along the paths of justice, giving wealth as an inheritance to those who love me, and filling their treasuries" (8:20–21). If knowledge does not develop into wisdom, then that knowledge is fruitless. The goal of education then is not to increase knowledge, but to learn to properly *apply* knowledge in the living of life.

Thus, the Western Christian idea of education has a component that makes it radically different from the ancient Greek form of education. The Greeks separated knowledge from practice. The idea realm had very little connection, if any, with physical life. The Greeks developed their scientific knowledge in the mind and generally refused scientific experimentation. They had long ago suggested that a large iron ball and a small iron ball would fall to the earth at the same velocity, but it wasn't until Galileo conducted his experiment that the law of physics was codified. The scientific method came later in the Western Christian world. Aristotle's *Rhetoric* appealed to a man's mind and emotions, but little was said about his *will*. The purpose of rhetoric was to establish knowledge, persuasion of the mind and emotions. Persuasion was not intended to drive action, only perspectives.

The Classroom

Recently I had the opportunity to teach speech at a local private school. I noticed that there were some students who were progressing well in the class while others were not. In an attempt to analyze the problem, I asked the students several questions: "How many of you engage in conversation around the dinner table? How many of you present lessons to your family from the Bible or lead study groups in your church or in other situations?" The result of this informal survey was exactly as I had suspected. Those students who were doing well were those who would take the skills learned in the class and integrate them immediately into real-life experiences. The home is a non-age-segregated, natural environment in which the young child may test his abilities without intimidation and ridicule. On the other hand, the classroom, as traditionally configured, is itself extremely limited in its capacity to integrate learning into life. It is much too sterile for true-life-integrated learning. How much of the rest of life is tied into a classroom? The activities of home, work, trade, and politics are, for the most part, not engaged in a classroom. Lecture-oriented classrooms have their place in academics; but when these classrooms become the pervasive environment, and when lectures become the predominant method, education will fail to provide for the integration of knowledge with life.

What Is Real Life All About Anyway?

We have defined *education* as preparation for life. If education must prepare a child for life, then we ought to have some idea of what life is about. About 90 percent of life is relationships, and about 90 percent of relationships are family relationships. Beyond that, the environment in which we operate in real life is home, work, and church. The activities of real life consist of developing relationships, raising children, conflict resolution, hard work, negotiating and achieving contractual agreements, debating political positions, visiting the fatherless and widows in their affliction (for Christians), designing and preparing the necessities of life, growing crops, leading, motivating, and delegating, and teaching others how to do these things. I suppose this is the most basic way of describing the activities of life. If education does not prepare us for these activities, if it does not teach us how to bring the principles of knowledge into life, it is all but useless.

The Bible teaches us to live life focused on others, not ourselves. It is a life of serving others. Jesus characterizes this life in such beautiful motifs as washing his disciples' feet and dying for sinners. This notion flies in the face of the "me-centered" age that seeks after the welfare only of ourselves or our own families. There is something inherently paradoxical in the statement from Jesus: "Don't seek your own happiness. You will never find it. Seek the kingdom of God. Seek the happiness of others, and you will turn out to be . . . happy" (paraphrased from Matt. 6:30–33; Rom. 12:10). As we apply the principle of life integration, we should incorporate this life into the education of our children. The visiting of a widow, the preparation of a meal for a sick family, an occasional missions trip, making a provision for orphans, defending the oppressed fatherless, and engaging in hospitality as a family should all be regular events in any paideia program in the raising of a child. Life the way it was designed is not cluttered, self-centered, and material-focused. It is not primarily technology. It is relationships. It is pure and simple—serving.

Integration

Experts in foreign languages tell us that the best way to learn a language is by completely immersing oneself into another culture without access to one's own mother tongue. In this completely life-integrated environment, most people can learn to communicate well in the new language in about three months. Otherwise, it would take a minimum of two to three years to learn the language, and then it is not usually learned very well.

Similarly, the first way to incorporate the principle of life integration is to maintain a life-integrating educational environment. When education is brought into the most familiar environments in our lives, an integrating influence takes over. This fact would commend home education because about 75 percent of life takes place in a home, in a family environment. This would also commend apprenticeships and cooperative education (where businesses work with colleges to provide on-the-job training experience to students). Years ago, I graduated with a four-year degree in engineering from one of the top three engineering colleges in the state of California. It was a school that boasted an intensive hands-on educational program, with laboratories in almost every course. Despite this superior academic experience, I will testify that this preparation was still vastly insufficient. For the first three years of my engineering career, I was virtually worthless to the corporation for which I worked. I made expensive mistakes and relied heavily on the more experienced engineers. It took me almost eight years before I could say that I was a competent engineer. From the beginning of my career, I realized that the only way I would become a good engineer was to work closely with good engineers in the field. Whenever I entered a new engineering company or advanced to a new position, I would seek out the best mentors in the division. I sat next to them in design review meetings. I took my designs to them for their review and comments, even though I may not have formally reported to them. I watched them and listened to them as they asked the right questions in the design reviews. Over time I became a good engineer and a competent engineering manager.

The second way in which a life-integrated education is obtained is by the provision of a great number of real-life experiences in the three-dimensional world. While some things are learned from a flat, two-dimensional textbook, most of these pieces of knowledge are not well suited to high-level memory, where one can recall them at a moment's notice for the rest of one's life. The ability to recall, integrate, and apply knowledge has a great deal to do with the connections that are established in the brain. The only way to establish a rich network of connections within the brain on any piece of knowledge is to connect it with a three-dimensional experience. Academic experiences beyond the books include field trips, experimentation, and handwork projects. This is not to eliminate the conceptual information obtained from books; but it is the field trips that expand, clarify, and solidify that information obtained from books.[2]

One evening last year, as we were preparing for bed, my wife was lamenting that our daughter Emily did not complete her English grammar assignments that day. After pursuing the issue a little further, we discovered that she had been working hard on a lengthy and detailed e-mail communication to her grandparents. It was right then that we determined we had become far too rigid in our academic program, and we needed to integrate more of real life into it. After all, when you grow up to manage a home or a business in real life, what are you doing all day? Are you busy working on English grammar assignments? Of course not. Your life is filled with things like writing notes and letters to family and friends, recording life events in diaries, preparing business letters, and maybe writing an occasional work of fiction, such as a novel.

Recently I have increasingly involved my thirteen-year-old son in my life. He is with me at least six days every week. He has studied his algebra, Latin, and English composition in my office downtown, in conference rooms, restaurants, the state capitol, the car, and on rare occasions, a classroom. While the environment changes, it is always real life. His education is much more than a textbook. He hears business negotiations in the boardroom, cell phone conversations, the hiring of subcontractors for a building project, sales calls, and an occasional high-stress conflict situation.

One afternoon last winter I received a phone call from a representative of an important publishing company. He was interested in a book I was writing and wanted to meet with me in a nearby city. I knew this would be a key meeting in the development of my own career, and I was tempted to leave my son at home. When he found out about the meeting, however, he asked me if he could attend. For nearly fifteen minutes I wrestled with the decision. Should I integrate my son into this and risk losing an important contract? What would the executive say if I brought my son with me into the interview? Would my son say something that would affect my chances of developing a good relationship with this key publisher? After all, one never knows what an thirteen-year-old boy might say! As I vacillated on the decision, another series of questions rushed into my mind—important questions, life-changing questions: "Exactly what am I trying to accomplish here? Am I trying to publish a book or raise a son? *What am I doing in life?* What better opportunity could I find in which my son could learn something about real life, real negotiations, and real business?" With clarity and certainty I knew that my purpose was to raise a son. There was no reason for him to stay home, yet there was every reason in the world for him to be there. The boy could watch his dad squirm for two hours while trying to sell himself in a high-stakes interview. So he came with me that day and watched and listened. On the way home, he commended me on several aspects of my presentation and suggested several areas that might have been improved.

By the time he is eighteen years old, I hope that my son will have the wisdom I have learned in my 20s, 30s, and 40s because he travels with me and watches me. He will learn the most valuable lessons I have learned in the same way I have learned them—through real-life experiences. I could discuss the principles of business negotiations with my son for ten years and put him through every textbook I could find on the subject, but real-life situations are far more effective than all the flat academic work typically assigned.

At all costs, we must avoid the separation of school and life. Learning must never be confined within the school walls for any young person. This does not mean to eliminate the two-dimensional, textbook work. But it does mean that if the student has nothing in real life to hang the textbook work upon, what he learns from the textbook will be next to useless and soon forgotten.

Think Integration

One of the most important lessons impressed with hearty dogmatism on the new initiate by seasoned teachers at home or school is *relax*. The tendency is always to load up the schedule of parent/teacher and students alike with quantity rather than quality. Yet so much of life's lessons are taught while doing life. Life is cooking dinner, reading out loud, playing a game, running to the store, changing oil in the car, driving in the car, talking on the phone, changing a diaper, visiting the chiropractor, reading the newspaper, subcontracting a job on the house, writing letters, negotiating, debating, attending a church worship service together, attending a political rally, bargaining for an automobile purchase, voting by absentee ballot, and a thousand other things. If our children know everything about the death of Socrates but nothing about the above experiences, they are much further behind the student who knows all of the above. The practical student will always know where to go to find out about the death of Socrates.

Several years ago, my wife was in the kitchen grinding coriander seed with a mortar and pestle arrangement, and the coriander was flying around the kitchen. Our little nine-year-old daughter Bethany looked up at her and suggested, "Why don't you use the pepper grinder for that, Mom?" For a moment Brenda gazed at her in amazement! "God has blessed us with a little genius!" she said. But how did Bethany come up with such an idea? Well, it is true that the coriander seed looks a great deal like the pepper corn, only different in color. Actually, the little girl was merely applying to coriander seed, what she already knew about pepper corn. This is true life application.

But somehow these applications come hard with education presently configured. It is as if we are learning to ride bicycles by studying "Bike-ology" for twelve years. We take Bike 101, Bike 102, Bike 103, Bike Statics, Bike Dynamics, Bike Accident Recovery Workshop, and so on. But we have never quite mounted a bike and started peddling! We have twelve years of theory and no meaningful life application. This is quite a stilted form of education.

A Fundamental Aspect to Life Integration

After spending most of my formative years on an island out in the Pacific Ocean, my family returned to the United States in 1981, and I matriculated into a large West Coast public university. My quick ascent to student body president there at the university is still an enigma to many. Looking back at that experience today, I can identify one key factor that contributed to my success. It was my ability to speak to every group on campus and relate to those groups. While other candidates were visibly uncomfortable in some environments, I was able to relate comfortably across the spectrum—liberals, conservatives, minority groups, engineers, sororities, and athletes. While being careful not to alter my core principles, I did adapt my message to meet the interests and the sentiments of each group I was addressing. Leadership, above all fields, requires the ability to relate to a wide variety of people who do not think and act alike.

A real problem with the modern classroom situation is the clique. Typically, the clique discourages diversity in the group, especially age diversity. The beginning of the clique is age-segregated classes. Often the clique narrows to income class, cultural background, or skin color. Since the advent of the large public school (which replaced the one-room schoolhouse), age segregation has become almost the universal approach used in school, church, and youth club. But as the young person moves into the business world, he simply cannot expect his employer to populate his division only with those who belong to his particular peer group. Unfortunately, this typical classroom approach also tends to encourage immaturity. The sad consequence of children growing up without regular social contact with those older than themselves is usually a delay in maturity. They are unable to mature in their vocabulary, relationships, and practical wisdom.

While growing up, I had the advantage of regular contact with people who were not my age. I was a middle child of six, and there were adults in close contact with me constantly. Also, I was raised in Japan, a situation that provided me regular contact with people from a totally different cultural background than my own. Most children who are raised expecting that they will always be associating with those who think and act just like them are not being raised to be effective leaders, team coordinators, or even team players in the corporate world, the church, or the family.

While the one-room schoolhouse may not be available to every parent, this principle of cross-age contact is an important factor in the education equation. Some children attending age-segregated classes *do* find creative ways to cross the barriers. Older children may be called upon at times to mentor younger children in another class. Some parents have more interaction with their children than others. Some parents intentionally invite interesting people with diverse backgrounds to their homes for dinner. (Our family had the privilege of entertaining a pastor from Zambia for an entire week last year.) Still other parents involve their children in their businesses on the weekends and during the summer months. There are literally thousands of ways in which we can integrate our children into our lives, our homes, and our businesses. The challenge for every parent is to find the best ways to make that happen.

The Loss of Life Integration

With the progressive advent of institutionalized schooling, the opportunity for life integration has gradually dissipated in education in Europe, America, and the Far East. Schools have been increasingly separated from family, business, church, community service, and the rest of what constitutes real life. Far more time is spent in a school building today than was spent in the classroom in the year 1776. Even by the 1880s, the farmer boy Almanzo Wilder (from *Little House on the Prairie*), spent less time per day, fewer days per year, and fewer years altogether in school than children do today. Yet it was rare to find illiteracy in America in the nineteenth century. The illiteracy problem is far worse today even though we now have far more professional teachers, far more schools, and far more time spent in those schools. In the seventeenth and eighteenth centuries, it would have been the exception for a boy not to have found his way into an apprenticeship by the time he was fifteen or sixteen. Now in the twenty-first century, hamstrung by child labor laws, mandatory attendance laws, and social expectations, it is rare to find young men at fifteen or sixteen who are seriously engaged in an apprenticeship. The nineteenth-century humorist Mark Twain warned of the potential damage that could be done by the institutionalization of education, quipping, "Never let school get in the way of a good education."

A Few Tips

This book is not intended to provide a narrow set of rules by which one might educate one's children. The broad principles are here. Therefore, the following tips are only *suggestions* that might be helpful as you work this principle of life integration into your child's education:

1. Tie in the things they have learned recently to what you are doing. If, for example, your son has recently studied the relationship of velocity, distance, and time, have him calculate your velocity by

timing between mile markers on the road. This means that you must have an idea of what your children are studying in order to incorporate that knowledge into real life.

2. Limit the time they spend listening to lectures.

3. Do things in life that are really important. Build relationships. The Bible gives us an idea of what constitutes the important things of life.

4. Take your children with you on shopping trips, business trips, and recreational activities as often as you can.

5. Train your children to think and communicate all the time, especially when it comes to the real things of life, the important things of life. Do this by example. The dinner table should buzz with intelligent conversation on stimulating topics.

6. Train your children to be able to interact well with people who do not think and act just like they do.

7. Encourage your children to start their own business or work the family business with you. Seek out apprenticeships, especially those that will coalesce with your child's calling in life.

8. Prefer hands-on training to any other form of education, if it is at all practical.

9. Look for a learning environment that is as close to real life as you can find.

10. Incorporate curriculum that understands the importance of real-life application.

Conclusion

More than anything else, life is real people and the contact that our children have with them. Real life is relationships, as we work to cultivate and maintain those relationships These include business, family, church, and social relationships. It is the development of understanding and love. It is communication and the conflict resolution skills necessary to guide those relationships through the rocky waters of life. A complex skill set such as this cannot be learned in a peer group, but it can be learned in an integrated family, church, or similar social environment.

Therefore, in the all-important task of educating the next generation, our children must be able to integrate the knowledge they attain from books into real life. They must be able to apply the concepts of mathematics, language arts, geography, history, art, and so forth in everyday life. Any education that does not provide application or the savvy for application is useless. Application must be so folded into the theory that it would be almost impossible to distinguish the seams.

10 The Eighth Time-Tested Secret for a Successful Education:
Maintaining the Honor and Mystique of Learning

I remember the first time I walked into a library. Up to that point in my life, I had never been in a public library. As a boy homeschooled on the Southern Island of Kyushu in Japan, I had poured over all the books in our own family library, including large portions of the family encyclopedia set. But this large public-access library was an experience of indescribable delight to a ten-year-old boy. Suddenly, the endless possibilities for learning and exploration snapped into my consciousness, and excitement practically overwhelmed me. It took my breath away to see all those books. Somehow along the way, I had gained a strong sense of the mystique and adventure that belongs to the discovery process we call *learning*.

The Eighth Time-Tested Secret for a Successful Education: Maintaining the Honor and Mystique of Learning

Sadly, the adventure of learning is seldom seen in the faces of most schoolchildren. There may be fleeting moments of interest, but school is generally considered "boring" by a significant majority of those who attend. This perspective seems to be shared by many junior college and university students. Many students find far more reward in the pursuit of extracurricular interests than they do in their academic studies.

Part of the problem lies in the rejection of the principle of individuality in our modern approaches to schooling. If all children in a given class are expected to perform equally well in all subjects (and they do not); and if some children are frustrated when they do not achieve the standard, and others are bored because they are far ahead of the standard; then, there is a strong possibility that a great number of the students in that classroom will have lost any sense of the honor of learning. And that general dislike of school will spread like wildfire, the end result being that many students in conventional classrooms hate school. Losing a sense for the honor and mystique of learning in education is nothing short of tragic.

There once lived a man who asked God for wisdom, and God granted his request. This man named Solomon wrote these beautiful words about the search for knowledge and wisdom:

"It is the glory of God to conceal a matter and the glory of kings to investigate a matter." Proverbs 25:2

The picture provided here is in the form of an analogy. It is as if God has carefully concealed certain things in the physical world of the rocks, plants, and the rest of creation. Everybody likes a treasure hunt, but only if we are sure it is a treasure hunt! And we believe that God has arranged a great treasure for us in his creation. The bush outside the window is not a meaningless, purposeless accident in a universe of pure chance; neither did it appear as a superfluous accident by a god who forgot what he was doing while he was creating other things like whales and roses. This world did not come into being because a chemist left an experiment too long over the weekend and then came back to a laboratory overrun with green slime.

The Christian worldview holds that everything has a purpose. God has a grand purpose for each of the elements, each of the compounds, each plant, and each form of animal life he created. There are indeed magnificent, significant uses hidden in the plants and minerals. This is the underlying worldview that has created the greatest poets, the greatest botanists, the greatest doctors, the greatest physicists, and the greatest agriculturalists the world has ever known. This is the worldview that brought up the tremendous advances of the industrial revolution with all of the modern inventions that now facilitate modern life. Many, if not most, of the early scientists, doctors, and philosophers from the seventeenth and eighteenth centuries were self-conscious, professing Christians. Their discoveries and advances all occurred prior to the modern institutionalization of education. Now we find the great minds of the modern age gradually abandoning a Christian worldview, while holding on to only a few remnants of the great truth that God created the world with order, meaning, and purpose.

The Christian looks at some random plant growing in the garden and he knows it is not random. It is no mere product of chance. The design is intentional, purposeful. In that creation of God, he sees the potential solution for a problem afflicting the human race for millennia, such as a cure for cancer or heart disease. He sees a potential fuel for rocket ships. This fundamental belief rooted in the consciousness of a human being forms the great motivation for all human creativity. If one believes there is something of value and purpose hidden purposefully by the purposeful Creator, then he will be moved to find it. If one believes that an intelligent Designer put a plant in place with a purpose, then he will be motivated to get out there and discover that purpose. Creativity is fundamentally *discovery*, and it can only proceed in a world that has already accepted purpose and design in creation.

This perspective of the world renders a wholly different approach to learning and our dominion work. First, this perspective realizes that knowledge is accessible. Knowledge awaits you in the next book you pull off the shelf. Some important discovery is about to break forth in the next laboratory experiment. Even knowledge of God and redemption is not inaccessible to the one who by faith reaches out for it. "Do not say in your heart, 'Who will go up to heaven?' . . . or, 'Who will go down into the abyss?' . . . what does it say? The message is near you, in your mouth and in your heart. This is the message of faith that we proclaim" (Rom. 10:6–8).

The great African-American botanist and chemist George Washington Carver captured a profound sense of this great truth. Indeed, it was this truth that inspired and motivated the man in his agricultural research of sweet potato, peanut, and cotton. The following poignant anecdote is told by Carver himself and illustrates this sense of wonder and purpose in the universe:

I asked God, "Why did you make the universe, Lord?"

"Ask for something more in proportion to that little mind of yours," replied God.

"Why did you make the Earth, Lord?" I asked.

"Your little mind still wants to know far too much. Ask for something more in proportion to that little mind of yours," replied God.

"Why did you make man, Lord?" I asked.

"Far too much. Far too much. Ask again," replied God.

"Explain to me why you made plants, Lord," I asked.

"Your little mind still wants to know far too much."

"The peanut?" I asked meekly.

"Yes! For your modest proportions I will grant you the mystery of the peanut. Take it inside your laboratory and separate it into water, fats, oils, gums, resins, sugars, starches, and amino acids. Then recombine these under my three laws of compatibility, temperature and pressure. Then you will know why I made the peanut."[1]

While that would not be the confession of *every* successful scientist, it is undoubtedly the presupposition upon which they must regularly operate.

God has created the universe and each element in it for a purpose that must somehow fit into man's great task of dominion.

Second, if there is a strong sense of personal intention and purpose behind the creation of all things, then this also implies that man is created with the *capability* of discovery. If there is something of purpose hidden, then God intends for it to be found! Man is created capable of thinking God's thoughts after him.

Third, this idea of significance and meaning in creation implies that there is a *usefulness* in all things created and our knowledge of them. In the beginning God created man and gave him the responsibility to take dominion over the world. This care and dominion extend over man himself, the animal kingdom, the plant life, and the minerals. That responsibility is still in effect to this day (Ps. 8:5–6). He did not require man to take dominion without simultaneously creating a world that would be of service to man. Therefore, the work of discovery is the work of obedience. It is doing what God has commanded us to do with the raw materials that God has given for that purpose. The work is not without challenge, but it has its rewards.

Fourth, if we believe that God truly created the world with order, meaning, and purpose, this belief should produce in us a "magical" wonder about the world that confronts us. The universe reveals not only purpose but a *personal* purpose and the touch of the divine. Our daily interactions with this world in the laboratory of the scientist and in the laboratory of life should yield a deep sense of wonder at the wisdom, the love, the magnificence of the God behind it all. In fact, I would define *romance* as a sensitivity toward the beauty, the wisdom, the complexity, the variety, the usefulness, and the meaningfulness of creation. Romance requires senses that are well tuned to observe this creation and a mind that sees the personal character of the message sent to us by this personal God. Romance is the feeling of significance — the significance of the moment's experience, the significance of the meaning associated with the experience. I do not entirely separate the emotional texture of an experience from the intellectual awareness of it.

Fifth, because there is significance and meaning in creation and in the revelatory truth of God's Word, there is significance and honor found in the work of discovery. The one who chooses the work of scientist or theologian or doctor or engineer or statesman is engaging a worthy occupation. It is a position worthy of great honor, the honor to which kings are due. Honor brings with it the idea of respect. The more one engages in research or discovery of God's truth hidden in his world and Word, the more he commands respect of others. He becomes an honorable man in the eyes of God and men. Honor, therefore, is not earned by affluence or wealth; but it is earned by the pursuit of knowledge, understanding, and wisdom. It is not so much the success of the search that yields honor to the searcher as it is the process of searching that makes the searcher an honorable man.

Finally, it is the great calling of honorable men and women to discover the truth hidden by God in his work and Word. This is facilitated by a universe in which there is the utmost divinely intended meaning and purpose in every revelatory word and in every plant and rock. Then it would follow that the work done is significant and ought to be done in a way that recognizes its own significance. All that is done should be done with all of our might. Such is the advice of the wisest mere mortal who ever walked the planet: "Whatever your hands find to do, do with all your strength" (Eccl. 9:10).

If the young student captures this sense of significance that lies in the facts of the universe because of the God who backs them, then he is drawn to study. The search for knowledge and wisdom becomes greatly desirable in his eyes as he enters the field of education. The pretenses of honor found in the popularity contests and superficial appearances encouraged upon our young people today should pale in comparison. True honor is recognized by and in the man who is busy engaging the pursuit of wisdom in God's world and God's Word.

Applying the Principle of Honor

Not much education will happen without creating an environment that virtually rings with the thrill of the chase, the mystique of the discovery, and the honorable nature of the endeavor. Education is not happening in a classroom full of long faces, empty stares, and bored yawns. There may be an expensive form of babysitting going on, but certainly not education.

The Power of the Mentor

The good teacher must convey to his students the value and purpose of learning. This happens primarily by example. Good teachers lead the thrilling chase of knowledge with the greatest enthusiasm. Almost everyone can recall a good teacher. The most amazing thing about good teachers is that they are found everywhere. But they are not always found in the best universities. They can be found teaching in kitchens and living rooms or tucked away in obscure junior colleges. They may even be found in business apprenticeships and corporate training programs. What can be said about good teachers? They are not always unusually intelligent. They are not always superbly original thinkers. They are not always found in eminent positions in the academic world. But without exception, the best teachers in our lives are always these who *loved* the subject more than they *knew* the subject. And the more they learned of their subject, the more they loved it. Their enthusiasm for the subject was contagious and pulled the students into it. They were excited about their field of study because somehow they had captured a sense of its significance. Embarking on the study was like setting out to find a mysterious treasure store. What exactly the treasure consisted of is not always clearly known, but that the treasure is worth finding is an indubitable fact.

The best teachers are those who engage discovery in the process of teaching. They discover *together with* their students. In the discovery experience, they exemplify and exude the sense of wonder, expectation, and honor that must be learned and shared by their students. This came home to me when I participated on a panel of experts considering the topic of education, which aired on a major radio network. One of the mothers on the panel held her Ph.D. in zoology. She told millions of listeners that she had learned more while homeschooling her children than she had in her entire doctoral program. I have found the same thing in all of my teaching in public school, private school, and homeschool. Teaching and lecturing can be the best way to come to a genuine understanding and full comprehension of the subject matter. Students will follow closely and intently when I am hot on the trail of an idea. The trail appears fresh and not well traveled, yet it is a trail that leads to something worth seeking. They can smell the adventure, taste the excitement, and feel the mystique of it. At times the students will begin to search themselves for signs of the trail even before the teacher gets there.

This principle explains that strange irony appearing often in education when a relative neophyte in teaching turns out to be the very best teacher of all. The most common fear expressed by parents who homeschool for the first time is their lack of experience in the subject matter. Somehow they feel it is a drawback to have to study the same material together with their children. But what they do not realize is that trails freshly blazed can provide the most reward for the discoverer. What many parents thought was their greatest drawback actually turned out to be their greatest asset.

This principle also ties into the principle of relationship-based learning. If the child's closest mentors exhibit a great love for learning and recognition of the honor and reward of learning, then the child will most likely absorb that same love.

Conversely, the parent who spends the few hours at home in mindless entertainment while encouraging his child to productive learning and school work will find little success in the education of that child. More is "caught" than taught. If a parent does not find great reward and breathtaking challenge in the facts of history, in a meaningful tale of fiction, or in the self-revelation of God in the Bible, more often than not his child also will be sentenced to the dullness of the trite and meaningless.

How can a teacher maintain a sense of adventure in the search, a freshness to the trail of academic pursuit, when he has been over the same material time and time again? The answer to this is found in the nature of knowledge itself. As it turns out, every time a trail is blazed there are new implications that may be discovered and new connections established with other fields of knowledge. New ways of understanding the material may surface. New ways to explain the material may also present themselves. There is no reason why the trail cannot appear fresh over and over again, especially if the teacher has come to realize God-deep significance in the material he is teaching.

The Power of Self-Motivated Learning

The student must also learn to experience the thrill of learning. Until this happens the student has not learned the method of self-motivated learning. This is a major goal in the process of educating any student at home or at school. The student must learn the thrill of the chase in learning. He must learn the habit of stimulating the adrenaline glands prior to the reading of a good book, prior to the exploration of any new subject area, or prior to the study of any part of God's great creation. Learning must be driven by the same mechanisms and by the same force that drove John Glenn to enter the space capsule that would orbit the Earth for the first time, the same force that drove Shackleton's men on that daring exploration of Antarctica. The student enters the study assuming that his discoveries *will* impact the destiny of humankind, that he *is* fulfilling the great call for mankind, that his efforts will be rewarded with some measure of success, and that great future value will accrue from his present investment. Ideally, by the time a child is twelve or thirteen years old, he should have learned this lesson and be self-motivated in his studies. This reduces the need for regular, hourly attention from teachers.

The Power of Peers

A student must surround himself with peers who have recognized this great principle of honor in education. Boys in particular can learn to despise school when the principle of individuality is grossly violated. This happens when they are placed in a learning environment and subjected to lessons for which their minds and bodies are not adequately prepared. In a surprising number of cases, boys are not prepared to begin regimented, academic work until they are eight, nine, or ten years old.

Moreover, parents should be intimately aware of the relationships that are developed by their children with peers. If their closest friends in the school, on the playground, or in church despise the pursuit of knowledge, that will inevitably rub off on them even as they are just beginning to catch a taste for the value of the pursuit.

Several Practical Tips

How does one nurture the spirit of wonder and honor in the quest of knowledge? I suggest seven ways.

1. *Cultivate expectation at the beginning.* The introduction of new content in an informal or formal education program must somehow create a sense of significance. First impressions are important. The first day of class in an academic year, the first encounter with the teacher, the first five minutes of a class on any given day, the first time any

material is introduced — all serve as opportunities to establish the value of the quest that lies ahead.

2. *Appeal to the survival instinct.* The thrill of the pursuit can also be driven by the survival instinct. This instinct is especially strong when it is understood that education is useful for life's work. This further accentuates the importance of the principle of life integration. If a student can know for certain that the present study will put food on the table later in life, he will immediately see the value of the present work.

But a factor even more motivating than base instinct is the survival instinct in the war of ideas. Occasionally I have found myself bored in the course of a study. I may be reading an assigned book, and the material seems to flow like cold molasses into my brain. Obviously, retention will be negligible. It is at that point that I ask the question, "What practical use will this material have for me?" If I can see that the book would be helpful to better frame a defense to some important position I have taken on some issue, then immediately I begin to see practical value in the study. Instantly I change from a disinterested bystander to the aggressive pursuer. That is because the purpose of the study has become clear. I must stock my arsenal of defense for the day of battle. If I can hold this purpose firmly in my mind, then my attention to the content, my facility for absorption, and my retention of it are all increased ten-fold.

For this reason, I recommend that high-school rhetoric (speech and communication) classes center on formal debate. Indeed, if done correctly, many or most of the liberal arts classes should include rhetoric in the form of either formal or informal debate. Forensic debate is one of the most practical, life-integrated applications available to the teenage student.

3. *Indulge the spirit of wonder and exploration continually.* If you see some strange formation on a trip through a boring stretch of road in southern Utah, stop the car, hike up to the formation, and examine it. Keep a pair of binoculars and a magnifying glass handy wherever you go. If a question comes up at the dinner table about the death of Alexander the Great, do not waste a minute. Jump on the Internet or grab an encyclopedia and *finish the quest.* Nurture the sense of curiosity, the excitement of the quest, and the joy of the find.

4. *Never discourage the inquisitive mind of a child.* Patiently attempt an answer for every genuine question produced by inquiring little minds. Younger children can be unnecessarily confined by the imposition of an excessive number of rules by restrictive parents. While order in home and school is of importance, it is not the only one of God's principles. Often parents can severely restrict their children merely for the convenience of the parents and thereby create a virtual tyranny in the home for a child who is naturally inquisitive and creative.

5. *Associate with those who nurture the spirit of discovery.* Two persons can sometimes employ the spirit of wonder better than one. One motivates the other and vice versa. One takes the other's idea and moves on to the next idea. This process of learning is powerful as the honorable quest is engaged in conversation, debate, and research.

6. *Avoid activities that mesmerize, yet do not encourage a spirit of wonder and discovery.* The heart of wonder and discovery can be squelched when a child indulges in mind-deadening and babysitting activities like videos, television, and video games. The problem with these forms of sensation is that the mind is led "by the nose" through the programs, and given little opportunity to engage in analysis,

imagination, and pursuit beyond the program's limited scope. *The child is discouraged from proactively engaging the pursuit himself.*

7. *Honor true achievement.* The failure to honor our children's accomplishments is a sure way to fail in child raising. While it is tempting to only attend to our children when they are doing the wrong thing, this approach fails to recognize and employ the power of encouragement and affirmation. A home where the wrong is condemned but the right is never commended becomes an oppressive environment. More often then not, children will become frustrated and will most certainly lose the desire to discover.

Some parents honor their children for the wrong reasons. Often children are commended for such superficial reasons as their looks or their dress. They ought rather to be commended for acts of courage, respect, kindness, diligence, and sacrificial love. On the road to discovery, they should be commended for creativity, problem solving (especially that which is self-directed), carefully constructed logical arguments, and self-initiated entrepreneurial projects.

We may also reward our children in the wrong way. This happens when children are constantly bombarded with gifts of little wholesome, spiritual, or intellectual value. When children are trained to think that entertainment is the highest reward and the chief purpose of life, their appreciation for higher values like discovery and dominion is dulled.

Achievement presents the prime opportunity to accelerate a student ever onward down the trail of learning. The Bible considers honorable those who discover knowledge and wisdom. Special honor should be attributed to children who do the right thing, the wise thing. Achievement can mean different things for different children. For example, a child with Down syndrome will certainly produce a different set of achievements than will a child with accelerated abilities in algebra and geometry. But each child needs to be the recipient of many warm affirmations from those mentors who are closest to him. When a child "gets it," the affirmation should be moving, enthusiastic, and genuine. Affirmations usually take on the following components:

- A recognition of what was done: "You just learned how to motivate your sister to obey Mom and Dad!"

- An affirmation of the value of what was done: "You have contributed so much to your sister and to our home. Thank you!"

- A personal appreciation for the person and their accomplishment: "I appreciate you. Your mother and I rejoice in you. We believe God is going to use you in an incredible way in your life."

- An encouragement to further discovery and action: "During tomorrow's family time, would you give us a short presentation on what you learned?"

The art of affirmation is essential for good teaching. A good teacher/ mentor must properly sense the right timing for affirmation and the right kind of affirmation for the particular student and situation requiring it.

Losing the Trail

We have described the quest for truth as a trail followed by the adventurer. Many forms of education built on the wrong worldview will lose the trail for the student. If a student loses the trail, he loses direction and the indispensable sense of purpose. Within a coherent worldview, the parts and the whole are equally important, and the one must not be lost in the other. The parts are interconnected and contribute to a whole. When the parts are seen as disconnected, the trail is lost. This is one reason why hard and fast separations between subjects are not healthy. When there are connections between the subjects and students recognize those connections, the trail begins to define itself again and this excites the learning process. Herein lies the beauty of the *unit study,* a relatively new but popular form of curriculum used by many homeschoolers and a few private schools.

Learning, as defined by a biblical worldview, is not sculpting. When a sculpture is made, you have no idea what it is at the beginning. It is not until all the fine features are in place that you can get an idea what it is the sculptor has been doing. Learning must be more organic than that, like a tree or a human body. When a tree is very small, we can still see that it is a tree. When it is larger, there is more to it, but it is still a tree. When a baby is still in the womb, it is clear that it is a human being. Its body does not have all the features clearly defined as it will when it is twenty-four years old, but it is clear that what is in the womb is a human being and not a dog or a cat. Even so with learning, we cannot present to our children parts and pieces of education and then wait until they are eighteen years old before they have any idea what we've been building. While we present the parts of education—phonics, arithmetic, geography, and spelling—they must see how these parts interrelate to make a whole view of life.

Imagine for a moment that you give an art class to a child over a period of twelve years. Your class each year consists of giving a child one square inch of a painting to view. He never sees the whole painting. All he sees are tiny bits and pieces of the painting. I cannot imagine a class more frustrating and boring than that. Educational systems that present disconnected pieces and do not present the whole are incoherent. Educational systems that present a whole without the pieces are arbitrary and meaningless.

Let us say that you gave a child the following pieces of an education:

- $2 + 2 = 4$
- Napoleon was defeated at Waterloo.
- Mount Everest is the tallest mountain in the world.
- God made the world.

But you failed to connect these pieces of information. The child may well ask, "What good are these isolated bits of information?" If they are not connected, they take on a kind of meaninglessness in the mind of the child.

How would you connect these? Here is one example: If God made the world, and God told man to take dominion over the world, then it would make sense that man ought to attempt to climb Mount Everest because it is the tallest mountain in the world that God created. Now there is meaning and purpose in those otherwise boring facts.

Connecting the facts into a whole necessitates a clear understanding of God, man's purpose, and man's redemption, even when our children are very small. The first catechism question we have taught our little children is, "Who made you?" By the time they are sixteen or eighteen months old, they know the answer. They begin to see the whole even when they are very young. They see how writing, mathematics, history, and geography connect with the Creator and what that Creator is doing in this world.

Once more this underscores the importance of life application in the learning process (the subject of chapter 9). We approach the whole whenever we apply what we have learned. Even our young students should learn to apply the tools of writing, mathematics, history, and geography. A child should be doing practical math problems as early as six or seven years of age so that he realizes the purpose or application of the theory he has learned in the textbook.

While we teach our children the parts of knowledge, we must regularly teach them how these parts connect with each other to create the whole. The method here is simple. First you move in and teach several small parts of knowledge. Then you step back and show them the whole.

The unit study is an excellent application of this principle because it attempts to pull the various subjects, such as history, mathematics, English, art, and geography together into one particular lesson. By this integration, the student can see how the parts relate to the whole. The parts instantly become "useful." This makes learning much more rewarding for the student as he traverses the trails of learning.

Conclusion

It is hard to imagine that anyone could disagree with principles of such basic importance. How, in God's world, could we ever pursue learning without a sense of wonder and honor attached to what we are doing? There isn't a teacher alive who would disagree with a principle of such enormous, axiological significance. The major problem with education today is not that we are ignorant of these foundational, basic principles. The problem is that they are pushed aside by other less important principles or erroneous ideas. This book is merely an attempt to reemphasize the most basic principles. Ignore other principles and you will not risk failure. Ignore these indispensable principles, such as the one considered in this chapter, and your education program for your child will suffer serious loss. These are principles that must remain front and center in our consciousness as we set out to construct a quality education and training program for our children.

Children are born with some sense of wonder. That wonder may be nurtured and trained. It does not take a great deal of effort to fan the flame; but we may just as easily douse the flame by failing to take into account the principle of individuality, the principle of character, or any of the other time-tested, eternal principles governing education. If we expect our children to retain a sense of wonder, why not enter into that world of wonder together with them?

The Ninth Time-Tested Secret
for a Successful Education:
Build on the Right Foundation

In July 1925, the world watched as two attorneys, William Jennings Bryan and Clarence Darrow, battled in a courtroom in Dayton, Tennessee, over what would be taught in the schools of that state. Eighty years later that battle continues in state legislatures, state school boards (notably Kansas and Ohio, of late), and in individual school districts around the country. There are few battles as intense as those fought over education. There are two reasons for this. The first reason is that the stakes are very high. Powerful interests compete over the direction set for the next generation. It is a battle for the minds and the souls of millions of children. It is a battle of ideas. The pen has always been mightier than the sword because the pen produces powerful ideas that direct the minds and destinies of men. As it turns out, education is in the business of communicating ideas. In fact, this is its major purpose! That is why education is on the front lines of the battle for the next generation.

On May 15, 1999, two teenage boys descended on a public high school in south Littleton, Colorado, armed with high-powered rifles, explosives, and handguns. When the massacre was over, fourteen children and one teacher lay dead. The T-shirt worn by one of the boys read "Survival of the Fittest." The Columbine High School killers were very open with the reasons behind this killing spree. On April 26, 1998, one of the killers, Eric Harris, made this entry into his diary: "It would be great if natural selection would take its course." As they planned the massacre, they maintained a Web site that included the following blog (edited of expletives): "You know what I love. . . natural selection. . . . It's the best thing that ever happened to the earth . . . getting rid of all the stupid and weak organisms." These killers held to false and destructive ideas, and they acted on what they believed. If we are merely an advanced form of cosmic slime whose purpose is to rid the world of weaker species, why not an occasional killing spree? Columbine is only the tip of the iceberg. Not everybody acts on these ideas in the same way, but a fundamental flaw in the way one views himself and the world around him inevitably produces bad fruits. Ideas have consequences.

There is a reason why the divorce rate is twice what it was forty years ago. There is a reason why the single-parent rate is five times what it was forty years ago. There is a reason why children from certain minority groups have only a 5-percent chance of growing up with both mother and father. There is a reason behind the 500-percent increase in violent crime in this country over the last forty years. There is a reason why children kill other children in bloody rampages in high schools across the country. These heart-wrenching social consequences are not some causeless happenstances in a random universe. These are real consequences, and they are caused by the promulgation of real ideas. The fragmented family, the moral decline of our age, and the social disintegration of the last forty years grow out of the dominant ideas promoted by both school and media over the last several generations.

All education is not equal. Parents are often tempted to think that choices in education are unimportant, like deciding on where you buy gasoline for your car. After all, it doesn't really matter where you buy gasoline. If you were to buy gas for your car from one company as opposed to some other company, it would not have much impact on the destiny of your eternal soul or your life, or anyone else's for that matter. It's even doubtful your choice of gas has much effect on your car. The same thing cannot be said for education. If the wrong ideas are communicated to your children, it will most certainly have an effect on how they live. If the wrong ideas are communicated to a great many children through education or the media, that could very well undermine our entire civilization. Of course, our children are more important than our automobiles. As parents, there are few decisions we will ever make in our lives more important than the decision about our children's education—how we will train their minds and disciple their souls.

The Ninth Time-Tested Secret for a Successful Education: Build on the Right Foundation

At the foundation of all human thought sits a worldview. All education, therefore, is based on some kind of worldview. If we seek a quality education for children, it makes sense to build it on the right foundation or the right worldview. There is nothing complicated about this word. A worldview is a perspective that is made of answers to the most basic questions of all. Take for example, the questions "What are we having for dinner tonight?" and "Who fought the battle of Little Big Horn?" Those would not be classified as fundamental questions. Basic questions are *big* questions about the most basic issues of truth and reality. Here are some examples:

- Does God exist?

- What is man?

- What is man's purpose?

- Can something be absolutely right or wrong?

As you can see, these are very big questions. The trouble is that not everyone answers these in the same way. Yet everyone has some kind of perspective on these questions. Every person who teaches, writes textbooks, or publishes textbooks has a worldview. They may not clearly delineate their worldview at the beginning of the class or in the preface of the textbooks they write. They may not be entirely honest with themselves and others as to the nature of that worldview. But that worldview will always inform the presentation of the material.

Some educators assume that God does not exist, that man is a highly developed piece of cosmic dust floating around in a universe of pure chance, and that there is no absolute standard of right and wrong. The education produced by such a worldview will be far different from that produced by those who assume God does exist, that man is created in the image of God with value and purpose, and that there is a transcendent, absolute standard of right and wrong.

Let the Parents Choose

Since there are multiple worldviews operating throughout our society, there will be different educational approaches available for our children. There are educational programs based on humanism (teaching that man is god), Islam (teaching that Allah is god), Christianity (teaching that the Triune God is god), and Hinduism (teaching that all is god, without distinction). That being the case, who will make the choice for our children? The reason that there is so much controversy over the issue of the origin of life and species (e.g., evolution, creation, intelligent design, etc.) on school boards and state legislatures is that these administrators are deciding the issue for hundreds of thousands of children in the state. I would suggest the best way to resolve this agonizing controversy is to leave the choice up to the parents. To impose a state mandate dictating the basic philosophy to be taught all children in the state by legislation or funding is a clear usurpation of parental rights and responsibilities.

The Foundation Is Important!

The foundation upon which the education of your child is built is vitally important. Choose the wrong foundation and the end result will be disastrous.

Such considerations do put a weighty burden of responsibility upon parents. There are bad educational choices and good educational choices that may be made. Parents need to know what their children are learning. At the least, they must discern the worldview that undergirds the textbooks. This means recognizing the difference between polytheism (all religions and gods are considered equal) and monotheism (there is only one God). Parents should know the difference between relativism (there is no absolute right and wrong) and absolute truth (there is a fixed standard of right and wrong); or the difference between atheism (there is no creator God), humanism (man is god), and biblical theism (there is a creator God); or the difference between nihilism (there is no meaning in history) and a providential view of history (God has a purpose that works out in history). Parents should be able to discern these messages in the way that teachers and textbooks present biology, history, literature, psychology, art, and civics. When it comes to education choices for our children, there is no room for errors as we lay that foundation.

An Inconsistent Foundation

It should be the desire of all parents that they communicate their faith to the next generation. Each parent must ask the question, "What exactly are we teaching our children?" Are they receiving a basically humanist education thirty hours per week and a Christian education for two hours on Sunday? If that were the case, the humanist ideology would predominate in their preparation. At the very least, the children would be receiving mixed messages at the most fundamental level of their education.

The Right Foundation

In his Sermon on the Mount, Jesus contrasts two men. The foolish man, says Jesus, built his house upon the sand. Although it appeared to be fine for a while, the house collapsed when the first storm hit. On the other hand, the wise man built his house on the rock. His house withstood the storms of life and stood firm. Jesus tells us that the rock upon which a wise man builds his house and his life consists of the words of Christ himself, as communicated to us in the Bible. We must build our house of knowledge and life of action upon the Word of God. If we do not do this, we will suffer the consequences in one way or another.

Many of us have been trained to think that the three Rs make up value-neutral territory. After all, would not a reading course for someone who holds to a humanist worldview be the same as a reading course for a Christian? Try looking at it this way. God is very important to the Christian. According to the Christian faith, he created us, sustains us, and redeems us. This is his world, and there is not a square inch of the universe in which he is not present. In the words of the apostle Paul, "In him we live, and move, and have our being" (Acts 17:28 KJV). Given this worldview, let us say that someone created a reading program that carefully avoided all mention of God. It is a six-year reading program without a single mention of God the Creator. The characters in the stories never recognize or even hint at the existence of God. There is no prayer and not a single recognition of God's hand in creation or his providential care of his world. The intention of the author is clearly to present a world without God. Would this reading program reflect a view of life and the world around us that comports with a Christian view of the world? Why should a child spend years of his life studying material that studiously avoids all mention of God? What message is communicated when the one true God of the Bible is utterly ignored, and even denigrated? The message impressed upon that child's mind over the years would be "God does not exist," or "He is not all that important," or "God does not belong in the area of the academic." This is the message generally communicated by most conventional, public school curriculum and classes today.

There is another sense in which neutrality is impossible, even in a first-grade reading class. What is considered *good* reading will only be determined by one's worldview or religious perspective. Is it a worldview that assumes order, regularity, and a creator God? Or is it a worldview that works to deny meaning, purpose, and a Creator?

Unfortunately, most academic institutions in this country today have carefully eliminated all reference to God in their science, literature, art, history, civics, psychology, and other courses of study. From a Christian perspective, the reality of God and his redemption is too significant not to be the central thread in the *paideia* or education of a child—the molding of his mind, his thought patterns, and his worldview.

I still remember to this day the deceptive lure presented by early childhood reading courses provided me at six and seven years of age. Even in the 1960s, the literature had removed all mention of Christian thought. This reading presented a happy and contented world *without God.* It was a world without sin, and therefore a world without discipline and repentance. It was a world without prayer, trust in God, and worship of God on Sabbath days. It was a world that did not need God and seemed to get along very well without him. In many ways, it was a false world. It looked much better than the hard, Christian world in which my parents lived—a world that was forced to deal with the realities of sin, even at the great sacrifice of the only begotten Son of God. It is hard to imagine that the ideas contained in a first- or second-grade reader could have lasting impact on a child's worldview, indeed on a child's faith in God. But ideas are powerful things. The worldview maintained by those who write the textbooks and present the curriculum does bear a lasting impact on children. Contradicting worldviews can provide serious confusion to young children and can result in an early departure from the firm foundation of God's truth. No curriculum comes from a neutral perspective.

It turns out that the Bible is specific as to the matter of the content of education. The kind of education or training specified in Ephesians 6:4 for children is "the training and instruction of the Lord." According to Deuteronomy 6:6–9, the education prescribed is that which incorporates his Word into every area of life (from academic to entertainment to everyday conversation): "These words that I am giving you today are to be in your heart. Repeat them to your children. Talk about them when you sit in your house and when you walk along the road, when you lie down and when you get up. Bind them as a sign on your hand and let them be a symbol on your forehead. Write them on the doorposts of your house and on your gates."

There is no other passage of the Bible that speaks this directly and this comprehensively concerning the issue of education. Much has already been gleaned from it. But the major thrust of this passage concerns the content of education. It must be literally bathed in God's Word. The revelation that God gives men is so important that it must be a part of the raising of children. The words of God must be a part of every aspect of the child's life. This is signified by every possible body position assumed by the child at any given time— sitting, rising up, lying down, and walking. God's Word is to be, literally, *in their faces*. The truth of God's revealed Word must be instantly accessible. It is to be as close to them as something tied to their wrist, as if it were hanging in front of their eyes all the time. They should bump into God's Word constantly, on the doors and posts of their house. Children should see the Word of God as completely integrated into their life experience. They should never get the impression that the Word is something they run into in some religious ritual on Sunday while the rest of their education, entertainment, family time, and so forth is completely void of the Word or even opposed to it. The idea that God is acceptable in a Sunday morning service but never in a geography class on Monday or in the car as we drive to the ball game on Saturday is a two-faced, dualistic approach to the faith. Children raised without the Word integrated into their everyday experiences are most likely going to lose any sense of its relevance for this life, and possibly even for the life to come. This principle emphasizing an intimate contact with the Word is reiterated in the Proverbs:

> *My son, keep your father's command, and don't reject your mother's teaching. Always bind them to your heart; tie them around your neck. When you walk here and there, they will guide you; when you lie down, they will watch over you; when you wake up, they will talk to you. For a commandment is a lamp, teaching is a light, and corrective instructions are the way to life.*
>
> *Proverbs 6:20–23*

This sort of requirement is the governing principle in child rearing. It must be foremost in the mind of each parent upon whom God has laid the responsibility of rearing a child. The Word of God must be tied into every aspect of our children's experiences, whether it be entertainment, history, geography, science, music, or reading. Children should be trained to think in terms of the Word of God. They should see the Word integrated into every subject of their studies and every aspect of their experience. This will not happen when God is eliminated from certain subjects.

Back to Proverbs

Returning back to God's book on education, it is interesting that the book begins right away with the very foundation of all wisdom and knowledge. After a brief introduction of six verses explaining the purpose of the book (to give wisdom, instruction, and knowledge to a young man), the seventh verse proceeds to introduce the most basic constituent of a good education for a child.

"The fear of the Lord is the beginning of knowledge."

The idea of fearing God bothers some folks because it does not sound much like love. But it should make sense that a father be both respected and loved at the same time. In like manner, the heart perspectives of love and fear towards God are not contradictory but complementary. Moreover, there is no way that anyone will ever love God for the love that He demonstrated at the cross of Christ, unless a person has first come face to face with the magnitude of his sins against God, which drove the nails into the hands and feet of God's only begotten Son. The atonement is meaningless to anybody who does not first fear the God who brings severe punishment upon those who violate His law. If one does not fear God first, he will never love God.

If the beginning of wisdom and knowledge is the fear of God, then one should never teach anything without this very basic foundational truth either clearly expressed or assumed.

What then would constitute a good science class, for example? Picture the instructor describing the order, the beauty, the complexity, the expanse, and the glory of the universe, the human body, and the animal kingdom. Then, he lifts his arms and whispers to the class, "Silence for a moment! All of you, stand in awe of Him! Stand in awe of Him! Let us worship the mighty Creator of heaven and earth." *Anything short of this is not good science.*

The history professor will discuss the bubonic plague that destroyed one-third of Europe in the latter half of the 15th century. But unless he turns around and tells his students to fear the God behind it all—the One who does His will in the whirlwind and in the storm (Nah. 1:3)—then the professor has failed to teach good history.

Incredibly, there are some who set out to teach character in the public schools, without any mention of the fear of God. What an incredible oversight that would be, especially when the Proverbs insist that the beginning of all wisdom—which includes all of the character traits recommended in the book of Proverbs—is the fear of God! Even when the Bible is taught in modern public school classrooms as literature, it is not taught in the fear of God. Or what about the sex education classes that encourage abstinence? They will tell young people not to avoid some sexual activity to prevent the incidence of sexually transmitted diseases. The message to teens is clear: Scientists are working on better ways to prevent STDs, but until that happens, it would be better to abstain except with one life partner (or maybe two). If the beginning of wisdom and knowledge is the fear of God, then the first lesson in every sex education class should be a discussion on fearing God, because he is the one who first wrote the words, "Thou shalt not commit adultery," and, "Be not deceived. God is not mocked. Whatsoever a man soweth, that shall he also reap," and, "The eyes of the Lord are in every place beholding the evil and the good."

What happens to children who have ingested an education over twenty years from preschool through university training, complete with 1,200 textbooks and 250,000 pages of science, history, and literature, none of which emphasized the fear of God, let alone assumed God as real? The inevitable result is that God is no longer much of a factor in their reality (metaphysic), truth, or ethics. God is a distant and far away reality from modern man. That is why the content of this chapter would come across as a bit strange to the average person.

What happens to a civilization that neglects to root an education in the fear of God over successive generations? Eventually, this fatal oversight will destroy knowledge itself. We have come to the point that scientists are unable to distinguish between the science that drops a ball 100 times, and notes that mass seems to attract other mass to itself by a gravitational pull (at a probability of 99%), and the science that takes a look at a rock and calls it 4,325,000,000 years old. With equal levels of dogmatism, they conclude that force equals mass times acceleration, and then they look at 600 factors that might cause global warming, and insist that the world will come to an end as we know it in 100 years unless we replace our SUV's with mopeds. A science without the fear of God will produce a hubris that can only end in irrationality.

As one scientist told me recently, "There is no essential difference between the science of Darwin and the science of Boyle, Newton, Pasteur, and Pascal." What a breathtaking lapse in clear thinking! Our lives have hardly been improved by the work of Charles Darwin, who left the world with an unverifiable, far-fetched hypothesis concerning origins. Such blurring of science and pseudo-scientific guesswork began with Darwin's hypothesis of species-evolution by a survival-of-the-fittest mechanism. While millions of scientists worldwide pursued this new pseudo-science with appropriate levels of hubris, others followed Boyle, Newton, Pasteur, and Pascal, and produced many useful advancements in the engineering and medical sciences.

It was Robert Boyle, the father of modern chemistry, who was insistent that we "remember to give glory to the One who authored nature." Before humanist science cut God out of the picture, Isaac Newton, the father of modern physics, would write, "There is one God, the Father, everlasting, omnipresent, almighty, the Maker of heaven and earth, and one Mediator between God and man, the man Christ Jesus."

But what happens to the minds of men who wander for 150 years without acknowledging their need for the Creator and His truth? Their scientists will busy themselves with worthless projects like extracting gold from lead, or acquiring clones from unfertilized parthenogenocized zygotes, or building towers that keep falling down. Science without the fear of God will, in the end, prove to be futile and fatal in a brave new world without God.

This basic constituent of a good education represents the sharpest difference between the Greek Classical form of education and the Biblical form of education. In his 300-page tome, *Rhetoric*, Aristotle somehow forgot to mention meekness among his virtues of courage, justice, wealth, and beauty. Yet compare that to Peter's three-line treatise on rhetoric (1 Pet. 3:15,16), where he slams home the importance of engaging in rhetoric with meekness and fear — meekness before men and fear of God. These are radically different theories of education. Unfortunately, I see little emphasis on either of these in most rank-and-file, speech-and-debate programs among homeschooling groups. In vain I scan through the manuals in search of any real interest in what God has to say about rhetoric. I would hope to find a chapter or even a paragraph on meekness and fear. The consequences of knowledge without the fear of God and humility before men will be counter-productive to the interests of the kingdom of God. Everybody wants to make an impact, and Jesus promised that the meek will inherit the earth, *but they have to be meek first!*

The Wrong Foundation

Given all of this, I can only conclude that an education built on a worldview that denies the existence of a Creator, that equates man to cosmic dust floating around in a universe of pure chance, that rejects an absolute standard of right and wrong is a *bad education*. Such a statement may sound a little narrow minded, but it would only be narrow minded to one who held to such a worldview.

If God created the world, if man has an eternal purpose, and if there is such a thing as absolutes, then it would be foolish to ignore his instructions. Certainly, to deny this basic foundation for knowledge would be a fatal mistake if you were setting out to build a good education for your child. To assume that God did not create the world, that man has no eternal purpose, and that there are no absolutes is to deny the very assumptions needed for logic, ethics, and science.

This does not mean that every other word of our children's education must contain the word "God." But it does mean that our children must see the connection to God in all they do. They must be taught to see this connection, and this will only happen by a consistent application of Deuteronomy 6:7–9. The Hebrew word used for teaching God's words diligently in this passage is *shinantam*. It is derived from a word used to describe the sharpening of a sword. The word means repetition, a "repetition" that produces a shaping of the mind. It is an education in which the basic truths are cross-referenced and reaffirmed again and again and again.

This also does not mean that we must ignore any ideas that are opposed to the words of God. But even when dealing with that which is opposed to the truth, there is still the connection to the truth found in the arguments formed against the opposing ideas.

Ephesians 6:4 encourages parents, and fathers in particular, to bring children up in the *paideia* of the Lord. Here, in this word paideia, we will again find the comprehensiveness of this godly form of child training that is required of parents. In Greek society this *paideia* was the process used to form the ideal man for the ideal state. Paul changed the meaning of the word significantly in his construction of the phrase "the *paideia* of the Lord." Paul was speaking about everything it takes to form *a man or woman of God:* "Bring your children up in the education system of the Lord Jesus Christ."

Two things are required to properly build on the right foundation of knowledge in educating a child. First, the child must understand the principles of God's Word. Second, he must understand the connection of everything else he learns to the principles in God's Word. Therefore, economics, civics, science, mathematics, and art must be built on the principles of God's Word. A good education will explain those principles and teach a child how to apply those principles to every area of life. This will equip a young man or woman of God to recognize and produce good literature, good business, good economics, good civics, and good science.

Civilizations that turn away from the eternal principles of divine revelation are doomed to fail. It may take twenty years. It may take two hundred years. But if we fail to build on the right foundation, in the end we will destroy ourselves, our families, and our civilization. An education that does not build on the right foundation is not a good education. When the storms come, the culture will fall.

How to Find the Right Foundation

Like it or not, God really cares about the education our children receive, and he will hold parents responsible for the choices made. This is the unquestionable truth of Deuteronomy and Ephesians. Since all educational methods and systems are not equal, parents need to know something about the educational choices they select for their children. Obviously, this is no place for a parent to be the babe in the woods.

1. *Know your worldview.* Every parent should have at least a cursory understanding of the major three or four worldviews that predominate the academic world today. They should know something about their own worldview. Generally, one's worldview is derived from his faith, but this is not always true. The strength of one's educational system will be determined by the choice of the right worldview and the *consistency* of that worldview. The reader may wish to refer to the publications of *Cornerstone Curriculum Project,* Dr. David Noebel, Francis Schaeffer, or R. J. Rushdoony for more grounding in this area of worldview.

2. *Teach your children the Word of God.* After all, if a proper worldview is rooted in an understanding of God's revelation, wouldn't it be prudent to teach our children God's Word? Moreover, God Himself prioritizes His Word as the core curriculum in Deuteronomy 6:7. If our children are better versed in their Saxon Math and their Shakespeare than they are in the book of Proverbs, the Psalms, and Genesis, than we have given our children a sub-standard education. What God gives in the book of Proverbs is his wisdom concerning truth, ethics, and reality, not to mention anthropology, soteriology

(the study of salvation), political science for kings and governors, business, economics, and other subjects. This is effectively God's book for the education of a young man or a young woman. It is God's curriculum. To ignore it, would be to despise God and His wisdom! The book of Genesis is God's book on the history of the world, and you will find it far different than the histories produced in the city of man!*

3. *Teach them the Christian classics first.* Some approaches to curriculum will intertwine the pagan, humanist writings with the literature produced by Christians, and thereby confuse the student between what should be the thesis (a proper worldview) and the antithesis (the competing worldviews). When a student studies a high school anthology, either he receives a cursory understanding of the great thinkers and writers in history, or he is taught that there is no truth and all ideas must have equal merit in the pantheon of education. When your child reads a piece of classic literature, he sits at the feet of a master. Before he listens to the ideas of a humanist, a deist, a transcendentalist, or a Greek thinker, you had better be sure that he is well-versed in a Biblical Worldview. Teach the Christian classics first, and then he'll have the wisdom to discern what is a false worldview.

4. *Think integration.* From time to time it is helpful to ask yourself whether your children ever enter a "God-forsaken" zone. Is there some subject of study to which they see no connection to God's Word? Is their entertainment an opportunity to escape accountability to the standards of the Ten Commandments? Can your children critically analyze books or programs produced from the perspective of an opposing worldview? Even young children can take notice when God's name is used in vain in movies or books, or when families

"forget" to thank the Lord for their food before eating. If you sense there is any specific course, hobby, or experience needing some integration of a biblical worldview, find materials that will make that connection for them. There are more books and resources written from a biblical perspective over the last twenty years than you will find in the previous one hundred years.

5. *Employ the principles of protection and wise progression covered in chapters 4 and 10.*

Conclusion

Most of this book is dedicated to the method of education. *How* do you teach your children? This chapter has more to do with the content of education. *What* do you teach your children? Our conclusion: Education is not neutral. The minds and souls of children are at stake. The future of our children, whether it be in this life or in eternity, is very much dependent on the way they are trained to think. Are they being taught that they are *dependent* upon God or that they are *independent* of God? If parents love their children, they will carefully choose the education that best reflects the truth about God and his world communicated to us in his Word. That choice of education is a parent's responsibility, a choice of the utmost import.

Jesus was right. If we refuse to build our education on the right foundation, one day our homes, our families, our economies, and our cultures will come tumbling down, like the house that was built on the sand. If we refuse to give our children an education that is firmly rooted in a biblical worldview, eventually we will lose our families, our churches, and our cultural, economic, and political institutions. They will drop into the ash heaps of history.

12 The Tenth Time-Tested Secret for a Successful Education:
The Principle of Wise, Sequential Progression

By the turn of the twentieth century, America was emerging as the greatest nation in the world by almost any measure—wealth, freedom, innovation, or military strength. There are reasons for this. In fact, there is something in the history of this country's educational system that is worthy of note. The mere fact that education stood as a high priority in the minds of the Puritans, the sons and grandsons of the Reformation, provided strength to the nation at the beginning. But it was more than that. This nation emphasized the basics in education from the beginning. It maintained high standards and wise progression in the achievement of the basics. Interestingly, Harvard College entrance requirements in 1643 included the ability to "make and speak true Latin in verse and prose . . . to decline perfectly the paradigms of nouns and verbs in the Greek tongue." Most students entered Harvard at sixteen years of age and graduated at eighteen or nineteen. First-year studies included logic, Greek, Hebrew, and rhetoric. The second year included ethics, politics, Greek, Hebrew, and rhetoric. The third and final year included arithmetic, geometry, astronomy, history, Greek, and rhetoric. It was not unusual in this rustic pioneering world of early America for young teenage children to excel in such a course of study. We have come a long way since then.

The Tenth Time-Tested Secret for a Successful Education: The Principle of Wise, Sequential Progression

It should go without saying that you cannot teach a child everything at the same time. A child must begin with material that is basic and simple, and work into more complex material. For example, a child's mind is not prepared at five years of age to study calculus and logic. What makes something complex is the combination of multiple concepts, laws, and facts at one time. As already discussed in a previous chapter, those that apply the principle of individuality in education almost invariably lose the idea of "K–12 grade levels." This, however, does not mean that a child at fifteen years of age will be studying what he studied when he was five.

There are different ways in which you may divide up the stages of learning. Most significantly, the Bible speaks of three different categories of content in learning, which can also be seen as three different stages. Although there is a great deal of overlap between the three stages, the later stages receive greater emphasis as a child matures. Three passages summarize the three areas of content for learning.

- Stage 1: "My people, hear my instruction; listen to what I say. I will declare wise sayings: I will speak mysteries from the past – things we have heard and known and that our fathers have passed down to us. We must not hide them from their children, but must tell a future generation the praises of the LORD, His might, and the wonderful works He has performed" (Ps. 78:1–4).

- Stage 2: "For though by this time you ought to be teachers, you need someone to teach you again the basic principles of God's revelation. You need milk, not solid food. Now everyone who lives on milk is inexperienced with the message about righteousness, because he is an infant. But solid food is for the mature – for those

157

whose senses have been trained to distinguish between good and evil" (Heb. 5:12–14).

- Stage 3: "But set apart the Messiah as Lord in your hearts, and always be ready to give a defense to anyone who asks you for a reason for the hope that is in you. However, do this with gentleness and respect" (1 Pet. 3:15–16).

Returning to the biblical book on educating a child, we find the proverbs distinguish three different words for the functioning and training of the mind: *knowledge, understanding,* and *wisdom.* These three are also combined in one verse that explains the preparation of the man Bezaleel to do the work of building the tabernacle: "I have filled him [Bezaleel] with God's Spirit, with wisdom, understanding, and ability in every craft" (Exod. 31:3).

In studying these terms in the Bible, we learn that knowledge is picked up by the senses. It is the memorization or storage of facts. Understanding is discernment or the arrangement of the facts. Wisdom is good decisions, expert counsel, and practical or technical skill.

Education's first stage takes place when a child is taught the first principles, often in the form of stories. They are, in his mind, isolated events in history. They come to the child as rules of grammar and language, rules of behavior, and rules of mathematics. It is only when he is able to apply those principles to the changing situations in the world around him that he achieves maturity.

The second stage of learning *connects* the principles and relates principles to the facts. For example, a child at six years of age may know that stealing cookies from the cookie jar is wrong. It takes an older child to ascertain (on his own) that a government official awarding a military contract to his friend at an exorbitant cost is also stealing. In this stage the student should learn to frame arguments against those who oppose his worldview. He should be able to look at the fact of something falling and attribute it to the principle of gravity. He should be able to look at the fall of the Soviet Union and attribute it to a failure of the Marxist economic system or its clear opposition to God. He looks at facts and interprets them in a framework of his worldview. When he is shown the fact of dead animals captured in rock layers in a canyon, he should be able to give the best possible explanation for that fact. How did those animals get there between those rock layers? Did it take millions of years, or was there some major catastrophic event that quickly moved layers of sediments over these animals, and then settled around them before they could decay? During this stage, he should also be able to identify good literature from bad literature, good art from bad art, and good music from bad music.

The final stage of learning is found in the application of the principles. This includes the idea of life application. We have already stated that life application is important throughout the entire learning process. It is even more important as young people enter the teenage years. One reason for this is that a twelve-year-old must somehow be prepared for life by the time he is about eighteen years of age. He must be able to sell his products or at least sell himself in a job interview. He must be able to argue for his positions and make a reasonable defense of his faith to those who ask a reason for the hope that is within him. He must be prepared to *apply* his arithmetic in counting change, changing brake pads on automobiles, or building houses. This is the time for the young person to prepare for life. This is the time to open his own business, budget his own money, and exercise basic skills of leadership. He must be able to make ethical decisions. When he was five years old, his parents told him not to walk in the street. But as he approaches adulthood, he should be able to work out for himself the principle "You shall not kill." He must be able to make principled decisions when he drives an automobile. He must be able to make the decision of whether to stop for the yellow light or not. He must know the value of looking for pedestrians and small children so as not to hit them.

The key passage addressing the third stage calls for the ability to give an answer to *every man,* which means every kind of person. The young person must now receive more varied experiences in which to operate. The homeschooled child who has been raised in the shelter of a home should now have some opportunity to exchange ideas with a wider range of people. This includes those with more education or less education, those with different cultures, backgrounds, and levels of maturity. These opportunities should be introduced carefully. All of this assumes that the young person is *prepared* to make reasonable arguments.

Applying the Three-Stage Progression of Learning

The application of this three-stage approach to learning is not complicated at all. It takes into consideration the physical development of a child's mind. The following is a brief summary as to how the three stages are applied to several subject areas.

Applied to Writing

In the first stage he learns the grammar, the vocabulary, and the punctuation of language. As his mind develops, he is able to relate these principles in the construction of sentences and paragraphs. Then he applies these principles in the communication of more complicated arguments and ideas.

Applied to Math

In the first stage he learns the facts of arithmetic. In the second stage he learns the method of algebraic and geometric proofs. Finally, in the third stage he applies the principles of math to engineering, surveying, economics, building a birdhouse, and making change at the store.

Applied to History

In the first stage he learns the facts of history and the principles of history. In the second stage he begins to interpret history in accordance with those principles. In the third stage he begins to make his own decisions, make verbal defense of his decisions, and play his own part in that history.

Applied to the Bible and Literature

In the first stage a child reads the stories and memorizes isolated truths in the form of short verses or catechisms. In the second and third stages he learns to explain these truths in his own words. He learns to identify problems with other systems of thought. He is able to perform critiques in the form of book reports. He should apply the principles he has learned to new situations and new areas of study.

Practical Tips on the Progression of Your Child's Education

Here are several ways parents can be sure their children's education is progressing properly. A quality education program will maintain a careful and wise progression.

1. Beware of the education program that continues to spit facts at students all the way through the high-school years and fails to address the final two stages. The kind of education a fifteen-year-old receives must be radically and essentially different from the kind of education a seven-year-old receives. The fifteen-year-old must be expected to operate in a much broader range of applications. He should be able to make some sort of an interpretation of the facts. Take, for example, this fact: "The American Civil War was fought between 1860 and 1865." A seven-year-old may learn such a fact, but a fifteen-year-old student should be able to explain the reasons

161

why the Civil War was fought and then defend his position. Was it slavery or state's rights? Or both? Or something else? He must be able to assess the facts, relate the facts, and then place them into an interpretive grid. He must also be able to employ his skills of expression to persuade others of his position. If a reasonably capable student is still learning the fact "in 1492 Columbus sailed the ocean blue" at fifteen years of age without any understanding of the significance of the fact, his education is lacking. How does that fact fit into a biblical view of history? Was Columbus a means of bringing white European oppression to the indigenous tribes of South America, or did he serve to pave the road for a future missions movement and an expansion of Christ's kingdom? If the student is only learning isolated facts and does not know how to relate those facts to his view of the world, then his education is stunted and incomplete.

2. One of the best tests to determine whether a student's mind is developing into the later two stages is to ask him to describe some particular truth in his own words. Ask him to explain how it differs from some other truth. For example, you might ask a child to define gravity. Or you might ask a child to tell you why it is wrong to rob banks. Or you might ask a child to define the Christian doctrine of justification and then tell you how that differs from the doctrine of sanctification. Or you might ask a child how this world came about. Then ask the child to explain the difference between evolution and creation as mechanisms for the origin of this world and its constituent parts.

3. The stages of learning should not be considered as completely heterogeneous or separate. A five-year-old child does, in primitive form, apply principles. He makes some of his own decisions in life,

but they are simple decisions. Doesn't he make his own mathematical assessments when he compares the number of chocolate candies distributed to him with that given to his siblings?

Speech communication is often saved for the teenage years, but it should not be *confined* to the teenage years. A young child should have continual access to good communicators, ideally around the dinner table. It is true that he will not neatly integrate important facts and careful analysis with good communication, but integration of all this is not important in the early years. Learning proper pronunciation, clear diction, a broad and easily accessed vocabulary, and adequate projection should be part and parcel of a good education before a child is twelve years old. Then the changes that occur in the education of a child are only in the area of emphasis. A five-year-old child should not be expected to draw very fine distinctions or make complex logical arguments. Likewise, a fifteen-year-old student is still learning facts even as he is analyzing the facts and applying the principles he has learned. On the other hand, do not overplay the second and third stages in the early developmental years. The emphasis in the early years should be in learning the rules of grammar, mathematics, and behavior by repetition, reading stories, enjoying music, and real-life experiences. The emphasis in the later years should shift toward analyzing the facts and applying the principles he has learned in discussions, debates, writing, expression in music and art, and in his daily life.

4. Take into account the principle of individuality in the progression of a successful education program (see chapter 6 for a complete discussion on this important methodologist factor).

5. Maintain a focus on doing the basics well. As a student approaches the teenage years, he should be writing at least a page a day. He should be reading the best books ever written and be able to respond to them in verbal discussion and written assignment. There is a

tendency to multiply subjects upon the back of the older student. This is not always wise. Continue with the basics, but only provide the student with more advanced and particularized fields of study in math, science, and social studies as these subjects fit the calling that it appears God has on the student's life.

6. The third stage of learning has a great deal to do with the student's calling. A student must be able to apply the things he has learned and his abilities to read, write, think, and speak to some particular field of work. Serious efforts must be applied to identifying that calling through career testing, apprenticeships, work experience, home businesses, and research. The young woman who is looking toward a home-centered life must also prepare herself to properly manage that household and cultivate her own God-given skills and interests. This may include training in law, engineering, accounting, education, or medicine, any of which could complement a home business in those fields of endeavor. The teen years are busy years as we prepare our children for the essentials of life: work, marriage, managing finances, and leadership. Any well-educated young person will be prepared to work a forty-hour week in some particular trade (even if it is home-based).

Conclusion

Two glaring mistakes can be made in the progression of a child's education. Either a child never learns the basic building blocks for future learning, or a child never progresses beyond the first step towards critical thinking and wise, independent problem solving. In the first case, the principle of individuality is violated, and in the second case, we fail to advance a child's education to its completion. In either case, the preparation of that child for life will be a failure.

A Vision for Your Family 13

O ne slushy February evening in Denver, I was driving directly into the sun. A thin coating of dried dirt layered my windshield. The scarcity of my windshield cleaner exasperated my desperation. At this point, I had all but lost sight of what was in front of me. It was then that it occurred to me that *you simply cannot drive if you cannot see where you are going.* (I have a gift for seeing the obvious.) The other thing that occurred to me right then was that a guy could get himself killed if he's unable to see where he's going. So I pulled over and wiped off the windshield.

This can apply to the raising of children. Put simply, raising children can be a frustrating experience if you cannot see where you are going. The consequence of raising children without vision can be a lot like driving a car without vision—disastrous. In the words of Proverbs: "Where there is no vision, the people perish: but he that keepeth the law, happy is he" (29:18 KJV). Put the word *family* in place of *people,* and you get "Where there is no vision, the family perishes."

Somebody once said, "If you're not sure where you are going, any train will get you there." That is exactly the way some folks end up raising children. If you have no particular destination in mind for your children, any method of correction and training will get you there and any kind of education will work. Unfortunately, when you have arrived at the destination, you may find out too late that you really did not want to go there at all.

Sometimes parents are led to trust the professionals, and they resort to someone else's vision for their family. But even this does not relieve parents of their responsibility for raising their children. It is not the village or the professionals but fathers and mothers who are commissioned with the task of overseeing the training of children (Eph. 6:4; Prov. 31:1–4). God has uniquely gifted parents with the abilities to raise their children in the right way. It can be done, and you do not need a doctorate in philosophy to pull it off! You *do*, however, need a vision.

Where Do I Start?

The people who live in squalor, filth, and disease often do not even consider the fact that life could be any different than the life they have always known. If that is all they have ever known, then they are usually reasonably content to live that way. In fact, most of the time they think that they have things pretty good. Their problem is that they have nothing with which to contrast their lives. They have no other *standard*. The only way people can get beyond that sort of life is if they acquire a vision from somewhere else. They may meet someone who has found a good, clean life or they may read about it in a book. The motivation to change will only come when they can see a life different from the life they know.

One of the tough things about developing a vision is that there are so many different destinations and methods recommended by education and child development experts. Amidst the cacophony of voices, there is one that I recommend above all others. Since God made the world, designed the family, and wrote the manual on life, it seems that it would be best to start with God's Word to develop a vision for the family. The key verse mentioned on page 188, taken from Proverbs, ends with "he who keeps the law, will be happy."

Also remember that Jesus recommended to wise men that they build their lives upon the rock of his words. This is where we, too, must begin to build a vision for our families. Regardless of where we are in time and space or how advanced or degenerated a culture becomes, there is always a standard against which we can compare the standards and conditions of the culture. The Bible has stood for thousands of years and will be that standard until the end of time.

Without getting into too much detail about how the Bible can clarify a vision for our families, there are two points I would make. First, God has a vision for your family! At one point in the Bible, the Lord provides a clear expression of his vision for a husband and wife. Paraphrased, he says, "I put you two together, because I want a godly offspring" (Mal. 2:15). There is no question about what God is after in the great mission of cultivating a family. He wants godly children. And God's vision should be our vision. Second, that vision should be defined more by the book of Proverbs than by the United States Department of Education. As parents, we can get a picture of what those children should look like at eighteen years of age. That picture is distinctly clarified by the character lessons of Proverbs and all of Scripture.

Set Your Sights High

Recently I caught a bumper sticker obviously contending with those who like to promote their children's achievements on the rear end of their vehicles. It read, "My son is inmate of the month at the county jail!" Sometimes our vision is limited by the culture in which we live. We might think we have lifted our sights, when we have only chosen the best of the worst. Generally, our expectations are set too low. No parent wants his child to grow up addicted to some narcotic or lodging in the local penitentiary, but *that* cannot be the extent of your vision for your children.

Your vision for life will roughly equate to your accomplishments in life. Caring, visionary parents will most definitely want to go beyond the culture to identify their goals and clarify their vision. The statistics show a steady decline in academics, public morality, solidarity of the family, integrity in business, and the work ethic. The current state of Western culture simply cannot produce a vision of a "godly offspring," let alone a vision that reaches for excellence in all areas of life. We must develop higher standards for character, marriage, interpersonal relationships, conflict resolution, manners, faith, self-discipline, and academics.

Vision in child-rearing has a lot to do with what you want to see after eighteen years of pouring tears, love, and hard work into your children. Sometimes I try to picture what our children will look like in ten years or twenty years. I picture men and women of strength, integrity, and faith. Once we can get a picture for what we are shooting, then we go to work.

A Vision of Victory

A good many folks would be happy if their children just survived their growing-up years. If the children could just make it out of high school without a drug addiction, an out-of-wedlock pregnancy, or a dysfunctional relationship, then these parents think they have achieved success. But we're not looking for mere survival for our children. As parents, we need to press forward and set our sights on all-out victory. I want my children to be conquerors for Christ: "Since the weapons of our warfare are not fleshly, but are powerful through God for the demolition of strongholds. We demolish arguments and every high-minded thing that is raised up against the knowledge of God, taking every thought captive to the obedience of Christ" (2 Cor. 10:4–5). They may not be prepared to do this at eight years old; but by God's grace, they will be ready at eighteen to bring down those ideas that oppose God's Word—and there are many out there. It also means that our children will need to be prepared with a robust biblical worldview to take on the foreign worldviews that dominate the culture. This means they will need a good preparation, strong faith, indomitable courage, skill in apologetics and leadership, and the tools of logic and communication.

How Do We Get There?

When a race car driver sets out to win a race, he will employ all possible means at his disposal to win that race. His preparation is meticulous and intensive. He checks the tire pressure, the cylinder compression, the brakes, the fluid levels, and a hundred other things. He trains his crew and practices with relentless consistency. As best as he can, he removes all obstacles and compensates for all possible hindrances to winning the race. And he does it all for the vision of victory. If our vision is to produce not mere survivors but victors for Jesus Christ, then we will use every known means at our disposal to make that happen. It will mean removing the obstacles that could get in the way, while carefully building into our children the character, the learning, and the worldview they will need to become victors.

Getting Started

This book may suggest a role somewhat new to the parent reader. The influence of a parent in a child's life is a hundred times greater than that which can be provided by any other person. If this idea is maximized upon by a thoughtful and involved parent in the raising of his children, this will revolutionize and revitalize the preparation of those children for life and eternity. A parent can begin implementing these ideas today by taking the following steps:

Step 1—Assume responsibility. The first step parents take toward a successful education for their children is to take an interest in it and assume the responsibility for it.

Step 2 — Cast the vision. The next step is to begin the process of casting a vision. At first the vision may appear a little amorphous. Over time, it should take shape. Put it in words. Put it down in writing if possible. In general terms, in a single sentence, what are you after in the raising of this child? Biblical imagery may be helpful. What do you see? Is it a mighty man of God? Is it a virtuous woman of God? A cornerstone in the palace of a king? Arrows in the hand of a mighty man? Negotiators with the enemies in the gates? A godly seed?

Step 3 — Spell out five to ten goals. Having stated the vision, you will want to break the vision down into more distinct goals. This vision, these goals, will be personal and distinct to each family.

The following is one example of a family's vision and goals:

Our Vision: Raising mighty men and virtuous women of God

- Our children receive the very best education by maximizing on the time-tested success factors.

- Our children are strong spiritually, growing in faith and character.

- Our children maintain mature relationships, are adept with hospitality, and are competent in conflict resolution.

- Our children have a firm understanding of a biblical worldview, especially as it applies to science, ethics, education, economics, and civil government.

- Our children are not merely survivors in this world but conquerors, especially in the realm of ideas.

- Our children are competent thinkers and communicators, fully able to defend their faith.

- Our children are fitted for life, work, marriage, and managing a home.

- Our children are fitted for some level of leadership.

Writing out your goals and posting them somewhere in the house can be a great way to objectively live out that vision. A parent may wish to lay out goals on an annual basis as well. Our goals should include far more than the academic and take into account character issues and the other elements of a good education laid out in this book. These annual goals are written *specifically* for each child. Inevitably, each child will have his own unique areas of academic and character challenges with which he struggles.

Step 4 — Convey your expectations to your children. Something I learned early on is that children tend to reach for and achieve the expectations laid on them by their parents. In fact, it is surprising to see how powerful a part a parent's expectations play upon a child's view of himself and his potential. Our expectations, of course, are based upon what we know about our children. Most of us tend to shoot a little low in our expectations. So I would recommend setting high expectations; and if they do not achieve all of them, be sure to commend them for what they have accomplished.

Step 5 — Plan out each successive year in terms of those goals. How will your choices for education, family devotions, entertainment, friendships, extra-curricular activities, and church work together to meet the goals you have laid out for each of your children?

Clarifying the Vision

Even after you have spelled out a set of goals, the job is not complete. It is still difficult to retain a vision for the family. The vision can get lost in the confusion of voices in the world or in the hustle and bustle of modern life, or in the frustration of being imperfect and having to interact with imperfect spouses and children! As with dirty windshields on Denver's slushy streets in February, if you are losing your vision, sometimes you need to pull over and clean your windshield. That is why it is a good idea to surround yourself with many counselors and read good books on the family. Most important, seek out the vision in the pages of the old Book, God's Word, the Bible.

Success also has a great deal to do with "how bad you want it." Is the vision something you could take or leave, or has it come to burn in your heart and run in your veins? The success of the venture has a great deal to do with the force of the vision. How much do you want a godly seed? How much do you want those sharp arrows and polished stones? It may come down to how important those children are to us. As we examine our perspective in light of these questions, the issue becomes even more potently personal and religious. Are these children really a gift from God? Does God have an interest in them? Do I have an interest in God? Do I see meaning in history, in the generations of my children, as an expression of a kingdom that will never die?

Conclusion

A journey begins with a destination in mind. You may not have the whole road map in front of you, but you should know approximately where you are headed before you set out on the journey. Attempting to educate and train children without a purpose, without a vision, and without an understanding of the principles that govern that process is a sure way to fail. Success will come when we are headed in the right direction and we take one step at a time in that direction. It may be slow and painful at times. But if our mission is right, we can move ahead with faith and confidence, counting on the blessing of God.

A Successful Education 14
for Your Child

S everal years ago, we received a brochure from a local private school, authored by a gentleman whose doctoral credentials in the field of education were prominently displayed. The good doctor explained,

> *"There is a misjudgment among some circles that a teacher does not need to be university trained or carry the appropriate credentials... unqualified persons should not perform brain surgery."*

Such statements imply that the education of a child is a highly technical affair that must not, under any circumstances, be placed under the purview of an uneducated parent. But what can we say about the theory of education presented by the principles contained in this book? Is it possible that we have misconfigured this whole business of education? If the best education depends on the preeminence of character, one-on-one instruction, the parent-child relationship, life-integration, and the fear of God, what is it that we have been discussing for the length of this book? Perhaps it would be better to call this thing "discipleship"! From a biblical perspective, education is discipleship. We are incorporating knowledge into life and calling it "wisdom." We are teaching God's Word in the womb of relationship, as we sit in our house and as we walk by the way, and we are calling it "discipleship."

This is a far cry from the Greek form of education, reincorporated into the western world by Thomas Aquinas and others in the 13th century, when these university men separated natural knowledge from spiritual knowledge.

We are not as interested in teaching chemistry or even teaching the fear of God, as we are in our students *fearing God in the chemistry laboratory! This is discipleship*. For 800 years we have separated these things, but as Christians we must reject this dualism now and forever. For a true renewal of education, we must see 100 times more love between teachers and students, and 100 times more fear of God in the classrooms, and this will only happen when we begin to emulate Christ in His education program. It is interesting that the greatest Teacher of all never started a seminary. He never entered a classroom. He told His students that He loved them, and then He gave His life for them.

In my college days, I never had a single professor ask me about the sins of my youth, whether I was struggling with lust or pride. Not once did I see a chemistry professor fall on his knees in the chemistry laboratory, trembling before the Creator of this marvelous, orderly, complex creation! For it seemed as if worship was incompatible with chemistry. Yet even worse, I never had a professor at seminary address my tendency towards pride, easily detectable in my theological papers! A thousand censures on such an abominable system of education that we have incorporated into this western, materialist world! We have separated character, the fear of God, and life from the business of knowledge, and in the process, have destroyed education. May God forgive us.

At the end of the day, I agree with the good professor who wrote those words on the back of the brochure. Unqualified persons should not perform brain surgery. But we're not performing brain surgery.

When we attempt the *paideia* of a child, we're performing heart surgery! And, nobody is qualified for that! Without the supernatural aid of the Spirit of God, there will be no love and no fear in our hearts or in our children's.

Who Will You Trust? An Epistemological Challenge

It would be hard to find anyone who would disagree with any of the ten secrets laid out in this little book. In a sense, they are not secrets at all. They come as intuitively obvious, especially if you are a parent. Who would disagree that every child is an individual, for example? The philosophical foundation you build on is important. Education must prepare our children for life. It is hard to believe that anyone would consciously ignore such obvious principles in his theory or practice of education. Yet this is often the case today. Educators, parents, and teachers must begin to think in terms of these absolute principles for education and mentorship.

These principles are easily lost when they are not prioritized in importance. In the final analysis, the way we educate our children and the way we live our lives will come down to whom we accept as our ultimate authority. Will we follow Jean Jacques Rousseau, the man who left his children on the steps of an orphanage? Some will follow the guiding principles of human philosophers like Dewey, Freud, or Rousseau. Others will be guided by pop psychologists or the latest "scientific studies" with all of their inherent limitations. Even the studies mentioned in this book are just "scientific studies." The reason we accept certain principles should have more to do with the fact that God has spoken with authority and he is the source of absolute truth. It should have less to do with how many scientific studies seem to prove the value of God's principles. This commitment is basic to a biblical worldview.

Another way in which a quality education is compromised is to adopt one of the principles while ignoring the others. For example, some academic programs and curriculum will emphasize the principle of individuality but neglect the role of character and discipline. They become child-directed programs. Other programs will capitalize on the principle of doing the basics well, but they utterly ignore the principle of individuality. Hence, there are reasons to commend the various unique approaches taken by some learning programs. But in their zeal to defend one principle, they cancel out another. Each of these ten factors is critical and cannot be ignored. They all stand together.

It should be clear by now that education cannot be left to "professionals." As parents, we are responsible for making choices that *will* make a profound impact on our children's future. The position is a little daunting. Nevertheless, parents who love their children will want to make careful choices. It is therefore essential that parents understand the principles of a good *paideia*. You cannot go into the decision-making process blind. The last thing you want to do is randomly grab for the latest sales pitch or the latest trend in education. You must make well-calculated, educated choices. Take the rock-solid principles of education that are rooted in six-thousand years of human experience, principles that come from the ancient books of the Bible. Get to know these principles. Think about them. Incorporate them in every choice you make as you construct the educational program for each of your children. Incorporate them into the environment in which they will learn—their entertainment, their books, their relationships, and their mentors. Use these principles to judge the quality of an education. Use them when you make the choice of educational approach. Use them in honing that approach. And use them as a yardstick to assess the quality of each child's education all the way through those years of development.

The Choice

The choices you make for your children's education are more important than the kind of house you buy, the kind of car you drive, and the position you achieve in business. When it comes to the education of a child, you are dealing with the issues of life and eternity.

Today, there are choices to make in the education of a child. In fact, there are more options than ever before. Parents are faced with making a choice among many alternatives. Above all, they should approach the decision with a clear understanding of the *factors of success* presented in this book. It should go without saying that this is an important decision. When making a choice that affects our children's future in this life and eternity, we must take into account the foundational governing principles. Will the particular educational approach maximize on these rock-bottom factors and thereby achieve a high level of success for each of your children?

Before making that all-critical choice, ask the ten questions:

1. Does this educational choice sufficiently integrate *character-building?*

2. Does this educational choice provide for *one-on-one instruction whenever needed?*

3. Does this educational choice provide a *proper balance of protection and preparation?*

4. Does this educational choice provide for the *principle of individuality?*

5. Does this educational choice provide for *relationship-based education?*

6. Does this educational choice adequately address *the basics of reading, writing, and thinking?*

7. Does this educational choice provide for *a veritable life-integrated education?*

8. Does this educational choice continually reinforce *the honor and excitement of learning?*

9. Does this educational choice build on *the right foundation* for education, a foundation that assumes the eternal truths of God's Word?

10. Does this educational choice retain a proper understanding of the *stage maturation of a child's mind?*

The Bottom-Line Challenge

Here is the requirement for parenting: "Fathers, . . . bring your children up in the training and instruction of the Lord" (Eph. 6:4). The next question for every father and mother faced with that challenge is, "How do we best accomplish this task?" What environment, what program would be most conducive towards achieving the nurture-and-development program of the Lord Jesus? How do you prepare your child for life and for eternity?

Assessment

If these ten factors are what it takes to produce a successful education, it is safe to conclude that there is not a great deal of successful education going on in a good many schools today.

This country became the most powerful nation on earth somewhere between 1776 and 1940. The form of education that brought this about was a combination of homeschool environments and one-room schoolhouses. Those men and women who led this nation to its zenith were educated in their early years in an environment far different from that which we have today. The modern system of highly bureaucratized school systems and age-segregated classrooms is a relatively new phenomenon, not fully implemented across the nation until the early part of the twentieth century. And it has contributed to our decline: academically, morally, and socially.

It should be obvious that a number of the factors covered in this book can be very well incorporated in a homeschool environment. This does not mean they will be incorporated in the homeschool in every case. What educational choice could provide for regular character-building by the nurturing hand of a mentor for eight to ten hours every day? What educational choice best provides one-on-one instruction? What educational choice provides the most opportunity for a parent or mentor to protect a child, or at least provide opportunity for protection? What educational choice best accounts for the principle of individuality and allows maximum flexibility in the design of each child's educational program? What educational choice provides for a more life-integrated form of education? What educational choice provides for the deepest-rooted relationship between mentor and student? In many cases, the simple answer to these questions is *home education.* There are some classroom situations that might successfully advocate the honor and excitement of learning, teach the basics, and root the curriculum in the firm foundation of eternal truth; but a full *six of the ten principles* would generally be best applied in a homeschooling environment. The reader should note that I hesitate to make an unqualified endorsement of home education. This is because there are unique circumstances in every family's situation. At the least, every parent should seriously consider this educational option.

There is an irrational fear of homeschooling among many today. They do not realize that homeschooling was normative in the founding of this nation.[1] Millions around the world are going back to it. You will not find a classroom for children in the Bible. Instead, you will find it normative for a parent to be teaching his child as they rise up, as they lie down, as they sit in their house, and as they walk by the way (Deut. 6:6–9). What used to be normative, what ought to be normative, is odd today. That is only because we are products of 150 years, or four generations, immersed in a new form of education. In light of six thousand years of human history, this experiment of men like Rousseau, Horace Mann, Karl Marx, and John Dewey has been short lived. But the good news is: the world is not left in their hands. Changes are coming. Millions of parents are concerned. They refuse to accept a failed system that keeps getting worse. Thankfully, this parental concern is driving the free market in education choices.

This book did not intend to draw a box around one particular form of education and present that form as the only acceptable approach. There is a temptation to draw hard and fast distinctions between homeschooling, private schooling, and public schooling. There is also a tendency to define these forms of education in narrow terms. This, in itself, is dangerous. It may hamper the principle of individuality for families and individuals.

Homeschooling especially supplies the greatest flexibility to form and define an educational situation uniquely for every family and every child. Many families develop creative and unique educational situations for their children. They might mix enrichment classes from private or public schools with their homeschool curriculum. Some families have traveled the world with their children, enrolling them in a variety of classes, providing a huge variety of life experiences, while at the same time maintaining some semblance of a homeschool in a motor home or hotel rooms. One family took a six-month bicycle journey from the tip of Maine to the tip of Alaska. Not exactly conventional schooling, and one could hardly call it homeschooling. Bicycle schooling perhaps. Those of us who have been trained to think "within the box" might put such an approach under the heading of "harebrained schemes." But ask that family to take a look at the ten time-tested factors of a successful education. They might well conclude that the bicycle trip would incorporate those principles, as well as fit within the family's overall plan for the preparation of those children for life and eternity.

Making Sense of All the Little Pieces

This book does not purport to present an exact curriculum and schedule for the education of a child. It is rather the *principles* that are urged upon thousands of different educational arrangements. In our household, every day is different. More time is spent on the books on some days than on other days. Some days are more chaotic that others. The changing situations of life can bring a sense of disorder, but this should not cause us great alarm. At the end of each week or month, we simply step back and say, "How much of the last week or month was worthwhile for the children? What was the overall value of the experiences each child enjoyed during this time?" We may not have accomplished everything we had planned, but were the critical factors maximized? Were there relationships cultivated? How much knowledge was life-integrated? Did we maintain a proper balance of protection and preparation? Did we retain an excitement and honor in these learning experiences? Are the children getting the basics down? Have we maximized on the principle of individuality? Education should never be measured in the number of workbook or textbook pages knocked out in any given day. Rather, it is measured by the application of the broad principles given in the time-tested Source of all knowledge and wisdom.

Conclusion

Parents everywhere are now coming to realize that it is not enough to leave their children to the experts. Even when parents make the choice to delegate some part of the education of their children, it is still the parents who make the choice. Parents retain the responsibility of the decision. Then they must construct the overall vision and piece the various aspects of their children's education and training into that vision.

After taking a century to pursue rabbit trails in education theory, we have come to realize that education has far more to do with parental nurture, relationships, and character than it does with the right curriculum package, the right psychology, and the right academic standards. It has more to do with the honing of great character than with some great quantity of facts. It brings wisdom to a child whose heart is bound with foolishness. It shapes and forms according to objective, eternal truth, yet the process varies for each individual child. It has more to do with the responsibilities of parents than with the responsibilities of the state. It is centered more on preparing a child for God than it is preparing a child for himself or for the state. Education is a tool that prepares a child for life and eternity; therefore, it should not be separated from real-life application. Education is not life itself. It is not an end in itself, for that would be futile. Education prepares a child for a glorious and infinitely meaningful purpose of living life to God's glory in this life and for eternity (Col. 3:23; 1 Cor. 10:31).

Notes

INTRODUCTION

1. United States Department of Education, International Assessment (quoted in 1995 *Digest of Education Statistics*).

2. *School Reform News* (Chicago, IL: The Heartland Institute, vol. 6, no. 10, October 2002), 1.

CHAPTER 1

1. I highly recommend Christian Financial Concepts Career Assessment Testing for the young person seeking a calling.

2. Thomas J. Stanley, *The Millionaire Mind* (Kansas City, MO: Andrews and McMeel Publishing, 2000), 34.

3. Robert T. Kiyosaki with Sharon L. Lechter, *Rich Dad's Cashflow Quadrant* (New York, NY: Warner Books, 2000), 8.

CHAPTER 2

1. *USA Today* poll.

2. "Class of Their Own," *Wall Street Journal*, 11 February 2000, 1.

3. Lawrence M. Rudner, "Scholastic Achievement and Demographic Characteristics of Home School Students in 1998," *Educational Policy Analysis Archives* 7 (1999), retrieved 2/5/03 at http://epaa.asu.edu/epaa/v7n8/.

4. http://www.hslda.org/docs/news/200908100.asp and http://www.hslda.org/docs/news/200908100.asp

5. Brian D. Ray, *Worldwide Guide to Homeschooling* (Nashville, TN: Broadman & Holman, 2004).

6. Brian D. Ray, *Strengths of Their Own* (Salem, OR: National Home Education Research Institute, 1997).

7. National Center for Education Statistics—Special Analysis 2002, retrieved 2/6/03 at http://nces.ed.gov//programs/coe/2002/analyses/private/tables/tab11.asp.

8. *School Reform News*, February 2003, 18–19.

9. William E. Becker and William J. Baumol, ed. *Assessing Educational Practices* (Boston, MA: MIT Press, 1995).

10. Education Week on the Web 2002, retrieved 2/6/03 at www.edweek.org/sreports/qc99/states/indicators/in-t3.htm.

CHAPTER 3

1. Thomas J. Stanley, *The Millionaire Mind* (Kansas City, MO: Andrews and McMeel Publishing, 2000), 34.

2. Helpful resources are available from the following authors: Tedd Tripp, *Shepherding a Child's Heart* (Wapwallopen, PA: Shepherd Press, 1995); William and Colleen Dedrick, *The Little Book of Christian Character and Manners* (Wilmington, DE: Hibbard Publication, 2001); and Richard Fugate, *What the Bible Says About Child Training* (Garland, TX: Aletheia Publishers, 1980).

CHAPTER 4

1. Paul Overstreet, "Billy Can't Read" (From *Heroes*, 1989, Scarlet Moon Music and Fifty Grand Music).

2. Gordon and Gordon, *Centuries of Tutoring* (Lanham, MO: University Press of America, 1990).

3. K. Topping and M. Whitley, "Participant Evaluation of Parent-tutored and Peer-tutored Projects in Reading," *Educational Research*, 32(1), (1990) 14–32, retrieved on 1/15/03 at www.ed.gov/inits/americareads/resourcekit/miscdocs/tutorwork.html.

4. D. Morris, B. Shaw, and J. Perney, "Helping Low Readers in Grades 2 and 3: An After-school Volunteer Tutoring Program." *Elementary School Journal* (November 1990), 91:133–50, retrieved on 1/15/03 at www.ed.gov/inits/americareads/resourcekit/miscdocs/tutorwork.html.

5. Jane M. Healy, *Endangered Minds* (New York, NY: Touchstone, 1999), 91.

6. Ibid.

CHAPTER 6

1. Rosalie Slater, *Teaching and Learning America's Christian History: The Principle Approach* (Chesapeake, VA: Foundation for American Christian Education).

2. David J. Vaughan, *Give Me Liberty* (Nashville, TN: Cumberland House, 1997), 32.

3. Laura Ingalls Wilder, *These Happy Golden Years* (New York, NY: Harper and Row, 1971), 15–16.

4. John Taylor Gatto, "I Quit, I Think," *CHEC Homeschool Update*, first quarter 2003, 18.

CHAPTER 7

1. KATU-TV, May 20, 2004 (www.katu.com/news/story.asp?ID=67497).

2. Will and Ariel Durant, *Rousseau and Revolution* (New York, NY: Simon and Schuster, 1967), 179.

3. Paul Johnson, *Intellectuals* (New York, NY: Harper and Row, 1988), 23.

4. *Encyclopedia Americana,* vol. 10 (Americana Corporation, 1958), 294.

CHAPTER 8

1. KATU-TV.

2. Edmund Sears Morgan, *The Puritan Family* (Westport, CT: Greenwood Publishing Group, 1980), 88.

3. Ibid.

4. See www.nifi.gov/fags.html.

CHAPTER 9

1. Paul Johnson, *Intellectuals* (New York, NY: Harper and Row, 1988), 10.

2. Recent brain research confirms these assertions as well. The reader is directed to these helpful resources: Geoffrey Caine and Renate Nummela Caine, *Making Connections: Teaching and the Human Brain* (Alexandria, VA: ASCD, 1991) and Pierce J. Howard, *The Owner's Manual for the Brain — Everyday Applications from Mind-Brain Research* (Austin, TX: Leornian Press, 1994).

CHAPTER 10

1. Rackham Holt, *George Washington Carver: An American Biography* (New York, NY: Doubleday, Doran and Company), 1943.

CHAPTER 14

1. Famous early Americans who were homeschooled include at least ten presidents, among them George Washington, Thomas Jefferson, James Madison, John Quincy Adams, Abraham Lincoln, and John Tyler. Other key figures include Patrick Henry, John Jay, John Marshall, and John Witherspoon (Chris Klicka, *Homeschooling, The Right Choice* (Sisters, OR: Loyal Publishing, 2000), 159.